Daughter
of the Dawn

"*Daughter of the Dawn* gives readers a glimpse into a little-known part of Hilton Head Island's history—long before its name became synonymous with beaches, resorts, and tourism. Avary Hack Doubleday shares her personal experiences of growing up on the Island and gives those of us who never experienced it a chance to slip back into time to imagine a period before traffic lights, resort hotels, or even a bridge from the mainland. Her vivid recollections of her home, Honey Horn, will help us share its past with visitors for years to come."

—Natalie Hefter, Vice President of Programs, Coastal Discovery Museum (Hilton Head Island)

"A must read for all who love Hilton Head Island from one of the founding families. The opening poem, 'I Am,' sets the mood for a compelling memoir of family, faith, courage, compassion, and a deep love of the Island."

—Nelle and Ora Smith, Authors of
Paradise: Memories of Hilton Head in the Early Days

"*Daughter of the Dawn* shines a light on a fascinating period of Hilton Head Island's colorful history. But this is no ordinary history. Avary Hack Doubleday is an artist with words, and the picture she paints for us is glorious, vivid, memorable. She was a child when her father moved the family to Honey Horn Plantation on the Island. It was a time when cows wandered into backyards. Marsh hens cackled all day. Copperheads sunned in the road. 'Currents and ebbing tides left behind deep slews' in which children played, 'little ponds warmed by the sun.' If you've ever visited Hilton Head, if you live (or lived) there—if you simply enjoy good writing—you'll love this book."

—Judy Goldman, Author of
Together: A Memoir of a Marriage and a Medical Mishap

Daughter *of the* Dawn

Daughter of the Dawn

A CHILD OF HILTON HEAD ISLAND, 1950–1956

AVARY HACK DOUBLEDAY

MOUNTAIN ARBOR
   PRESS
Alpharetta, GA

The author has tried to recreate events, locations, and conversations from her memories of them. The author has made every effort to give credit to the source of any images, quotes, or other material contained within and obtain permissions when feasible.

This ISBN is the property of Mountain Arbor Press for the express purpose of sales and distribution of this title. The content of this book is the property of the copyright holder only. Mountain Arbor Press does not hold any ownership of the content of this book and is not liable in any way for the materials contained within. The views and opinions expressed in this book are the property of the author, and do not necessarily reflect those of Mountain Arbor Press.

Copyright © 2019 by Avary Hack Doubleday

All rights reserved. No part of this book may be reproduced or transmitted in any form or by any means, electronic or mechanical, including photocopying, recording, or any information storage and retrieval system, without permission in writing from the author, excepting brief quotes used in reviews.

ISBN: 978-1-63183-539-1 - Paperback

Library of Congress Control Number: 2019905013

Printed in the United States of America   062419

∞This paper meets the requirements of ANSI/NISO Z39.48-1992 (Permanence of Paper)

Permission granted by *The Island Packet*, Hilton Head Island, South Carolina, for use of the photograph on page 158, and by the family of Aileen McGinty for the use of her poem on page 137.

Author photo by Marty Boone

For Ginny Hack Borghi and Kendall Avary Hack, my nieces, who grew up on Hilton Head Island in a time totally unlike the one in which their father and I lived

I Am

I am from Hinesville,
    from pine trees and hogs,
    from Walthourville and Midway,
    from a playhouse and a billy goat,
    from Presbyterians and Sunday School,
    from shelling butter beans for a nickel.
I am from the smell of salt marshes,
    of saddle leather and horse sweat,
    of scuppernongs and muscadines,
    of SweetHeart soap and Royal Secret,
    of Ligustrum and loquats.
I am from the sound of horses' hooves,
    of turkey gobbles and owls' calls,
    of lilting Gullah voices,
    of the surf's crash and sigh,
    of the song in the conch shell,
    of the marsh hen's cackles and buoys in the night.
I am from the heron landing,
    from the vulture soaring,
    from the raised white tail of the deer,
    from the rabbit's twitching ear,
    from the slither of the snake,
    and the fiddler's sidewise scurry.
I am from the colors of the painted bunting,
    of silver sunlight and moonlight on water,
    of the gleam of animal eyes in the night,
    of delicate petals of the wild azalea,
    of sea oats and sand dollars.
I am from the Island.

Contents

Introduction	xi
Memory of Home	1
Kitchen Mornings	5
Venturing to an Island	11
Getting There	17
What's in a Name?	21
The Lay of the Land	29
Barefoot Days	39
Life on the Creek	47
Horses for Work and Play	53
A One-Room School	59
Fuskie and Dellie	71
A Playground for the Rich	75
Kinfolks and Wild Birds	85
Sand, Shells, and a Wolf	91
Let's Take a Ride	97
A Fertile Land	103
Vanishing Paradise	107
Fire!	109
Going to Town	111
Easter Joys	119
Trick or Treat!	125
Hosts of Angels	129

Santa Claus Is Real!	137
Turkeys at Church	143
Daddy as Doctor	151
Hurricane's Coming!	155
Sunrise	161
Epilogue	163
Acknowledgments	169
Brief Chronology	171
Sources and Inspiration	173

Introduction

My life on Hilton Head Island, South Carolina, began in the summer of 1950 when my father, Fred C. Hack, moved his young family to Honey Horn Plantation. We moved from a small South Georgia town to an even more rural area. For my brother, Frederick, and me, life changed little: we still ran barefoot in our yard and played on our swing set. But horses and wagons, the primary means of transportation, passed on the dirt road beside our house, rather than cars passing on the highway. Mother cooked on a wood stove. In the field around our house, cows, horses, turkeys, and two mules ranged freely. Though we accompanied Mother on weekly trips to Savannah via a combination of boat and car, we didn't realize the inconvenience of living away from telephones, grocery stores, and electric power.

Also unknown to us children, this midpoint in the century marked a change in direction for Hilton Head Island. The quiet and secluded barrier island off the coast of South Carolina saw the first glimmers of modern development. The Island was inhabited primarily by small communities of black island natives, descendants of slaves. There were also a few oyster and shrimp fisheries. Large portions of the Island were owned by New York investors for use as a family retreat and private hunting reserve.

After Daddy and his associates purchased 8,200 acres on the Island to harvest timber, they also recognized the potential for development, and changed their focus. From that moment, Mother and Daddy, unconsciously, used a unique opportunity to help shape the development and character of an area, which to this day reflects their values: their commitment to faith, the natural environment, and service to the community.

Daughter of the Dawn is a collection of my memories of childhood before the bridge was built to the Island—with little bits of history thrown in. I hope it opens a new view onto life as it was before the dawn of the new age.

Memory of Home

My first memory of Hilton Head Island is of sitting on the rim of the bathroom basin while Annie Lee washed sand from my feet. Mother wrote in her diary that evening, May 24, 1950: "We went to Hilton Head. . . . and saw the house we will probably live in for a while." It's surprising that Mother, who insisted we always include "Island" when referring to our home, did not do so in her first recorded reference.

The following month, in June, my parents, Fred and Billie Hack, moved to Hilton Head Island and into that house at Honey Horn Plantation, which was "home" to me for the rest of their lives. Honey Horn is a beautiful name, whose origin isn't known. Supposition is it's a corrupted pronunciation of "Hanahan," the name of the original planter in the area. Fred and Billie brought two children, barely more than toddlers. I was almost five and Frederick was two and a half. Looking back, I can't imagine how Mother agreed to Daddy's plan to bring their young family to such a place. What a daunting adventure it must have been!

Hilton Head Island got its name from Captain William Hilton, who in 1663 identified a headland near the entrance to Port Royal Sound, which mapmakers named "Hilton's Headland." In 1950, it had a population of about three hundred, mostly black Native Islanders. There was no doctor, no church for white residents, no grocery store, no telephone, no electricity—which meant using home remedies, a large wood-burning stove for cooking, an icebox, and a diesel generator to provide lights. There was no bridge to the mainland—nor even a

Aerial view of Honey Horn Plantation. Counterclockwise from top right: the Armstrongs' house, our house, the Shop, the Taylors' house, roof of the Big Barn. The road and bridge at the top are the new Spanish Wells Road, opened in 1957, after the events of this book.

regularly scheduled ferry. There was one paved road running about nine miles, from the Jenkins Island landing to the Hilton Head Lighthouse, which had been built by the Coast Guard in the 1870s. All other roads were dirt or surfaced with crushed oyster shells. We had a Chevrolet sedan and an open Army Jeep.

White children on the Island—and there weren't many—attended a one-room school with one teacher. There were never more than seven students in these final years of the school. I don't remember seeing a black elementary school, though several were scattered around the Island. Segregated schools were the norm during the 1950s.

None of these inconveniences mattered to Frederick and me. We had no idea we might be missing out on anything. And it was years before it dawned on us that we had been transported to an unspoiled island, lush with forests of magnificent pines and ancient oak trees. The woods, marshes, and beaches teemed with wildlife. When we visited Daddy's sawmills, we saw alligators in the same ponds where the mill workers bathed. On the beach we stood on the backs of loggerhead sea turtles or marveled at prehistoric horseshoe crabs. On any drive along the dirt roads, we saw bobwhite quail, wild boar, ducks on the ponds, rattlesnakes sunning on the sandy lanes, and the white tails of deer leaping away into the woods. Sometimes after supper, Daddy would say, "Let's go see what's in the field." Slowly circling the car, he paused the beam of the headlights on a pair of gleaming eyes: near the ground, a raccoon or opossum—or rarely, a whip-poor-will; higher, a deer or, disappointingly, one of our cows; and the eyes farthest from the ground were those of a startled horse. In the ponds, alligators' eyes shone red. Spiders sparkled in the sandy roads before us.

Lying in bed at night, we heard the haunting booms from buoys floating, rocking in Skull Creek. Then came the *clippity-clippity-clippity* of a marsh tacky on the oyster-shelled road beside the house, followed by the louder thuds as the horse crossed the wooden bridge. Unknown to me, those receding hoofbeats in the night were an omen of the impending changes in the lives of those of us on the Island.

Kitchen Mornings

In Hinesville, Georgia, where we lived before moving to Hilton Head Island, the windows in our two-bedroom, concrete-block duplex were so high I couldn't see outside. The railroad track ran not far behind the house. Often, as Mother tucked us into bed, we heard the long, haunting sound of a train whistle and the rumble of the wheels along the rails. Mother told us a train wheel is so heavy that not enough men can stand around it to lift it. We loved a story in one of our books about a family's trip on a train, where they slept overnight in Pullman bunks and ate in the dining car.

I remember Frederick, sitting in his high chair, as I fed him. As a four-year-old, I got more Pablum on his face than in his mouth. Pablum was a bland yet nutritious cereal for babies in the 1940s. On the other hand, Cream of Wheat mixed with a soft-boiled egg, with a buttery, warm aroma, was delicious. Another kitchen smell was that of wild crabapples as Mother made jelly. As they bubbled in a large pot on the stove, they gave off an awful odor. Mother poured the jelly into sterilized jars and sealed them with a layer of paraffin. Crabapple jelly was delicious.

Our kitchen table was a drop-leaf one that had been bought unfinished and stained a dark brown. One Sunday as we were having breakfast, while no one had an eye on him, Frederick crawled under the kitchen table and unplugged the waffle iron. Sparks flew and his little fingers were burned black. We were all frightened as he cried in surprise and pain, thankfully not seriously harmed—but we both learned a lesson.

I had a special friend, Goldilocks, who lived in one of the lower cabinets. Imagining her comfortably inside, I opened the door, sat on the floor, and talked happily with her. Did that cupboard remind me of the Three Bears' house? Or did my Cream of Wheat bring to mind their porridge that was "just right"?

Right outside the back door of the apartment, Annie Lee would wash clothes in a large galvanized tub. She rubbed the clothes on a corrugated glass washboard in the sudsy, hot water, smelling of strong laundry soap. Annie Lee worked mostly for Grandmother, Daddy's mother, but some days for Mother. I was fascinated by the totally hairless skin on her left arm, which was as smooth as glass. It had been badly burned, but retained its dark chocolate color. This was a scar of heroism and honor: when her family's home had burned, she had rushed back inside and rescued her younger brother.

For a brief time, I took ballet lessons. These were vain attempts to teach little girls to move gracefully. During one of the first classes, for some reason, I climbed onto a large, wooden crate. I jumped back onto the floor and broke my right leg. Mother and Daddy quickly took me to a doctor, who didn't think my leg was broken. As the pain in my leg continued to keep me from walking on it, Daddy took me back to the doctor. An X-ray showed the break, and the doctor applied a plaster cast. Daddy had to carry me home that day, but during the several weeks I wore the cast, I became quite proficient on crutches. Frederick and I would race up the sidewalk—and I won. He, of course, was only two. Mother took me to the ballet recital, where I was so envious of the other girls in ruffled green playsuits. In one memorable "dance," they performed in pairs: one was a wheelbarrow, "wheeled" along on her hands by another girl who held her legs as the handles of the wheelbarrow. I felt it was so unfair that I had broken my leg and not been able to participate.

We played mostly outside. Daddy had a swing set and a playhouse built for us—both constructed of fragrant creosoted wood. Jim Ann and her younger sister lived next door and played with us: running through the sprinkler, making mud pies. Jim Ann actually ate mud pies and urged me to do the same. I took one tiny taste.

Avary (left) and Jim Ann making mud pies.

Avary in backyard swing, Hinesville.

Avary and Frederick in Hinesville.

Avary with her uncle, Orion, 1947.

Located on the outskirts of Hinesville was Hacks Pasture, a large piece of property of almost two thousand acres owned by Daddy's family. It was typical South Georgia land, made up of pine woods, palmetto thickets, and swamps. Daddy loved to take us there on Sunday afternoons for a picnic. Orion (pronounced with the emphasis on the first syllable: O're-un), Daddy's brother, raised a few hogs at the Pasture. They were huge, squealing, grunting animals, which seemed to enjoy rolling in the smelly mud of their pen. Orion demonstrated their size and strength by standing on the back of one.

Hacks Pasture and various scattered properties inherited from Mother's family both planted a seed and highlighted a symptom which still haunts our family. Daddy felt a special tie to the land, a value he passed to his children. A drive to acquire private acres to surround us led my husband, Gerry, and me to buy ninety acres in the mountains near Highlands, North Carolina. The other side is the "curse" of multigenerational and multi-family land ownership. Such varied owners of a piece of property complicate decisions: cut timber, improve property, sell it. No one is purposefully uncooperative or selfish. We just need different things at different times. Such inaction results in even more complicated ownership as new generations are born. We are the products of our past.

Venturing to an Island

At some point during the years in Hinesville, Daddy expanded the business of cutting timber from his family property and incorporated Hack Lumber Company. He then contracted to cut and sell timber from land owned by others. When at the end of 1949 he learned that a large tract of beachfront wilderness on the south end of Hilton Head Island was for sale, he made an appointment to see the land and evaluate the timber prospects. This was not Daddy's introduction to the Island. The story goes that, in 1922 at eight years old, he had traveled on the steamship *Clivedon* from Savannah to Beaufort to visit his grandmother. Riding on the top deck of the boat, he watched as the Islanders rowed out to trade for rice and other staples, and admired the beautiful forests on this island, whose only connection with the mainland was by boat.

On a deer hunt in Hinesville, Daddy mentioned to General Joseph B. Fraser that he had an appointment to see this land. The two of them visited the Island and thought the timber prospects were great. Based on this assessment, they boldly decided to purchase the land. They and a few other investors formed The Hilton Head Company and bought 8,200 acres for about sixty dollars an acre, which was a huge sum. This included most of the land south of what is now Palmetto Dunes Plantation. A few months later, in March of 1951, Daddy, O. T. McIntosh (of Southern States Naval Stores in Savannah), and C. C. Stebbins (Mother's father) bought another 9,200 acres, comprising most of the remaining areas of the Island which have since been developed, except the current Jenkins Island and Palmetto Dunes.

In 1950, Daddy and General Fraser set up three sawmills on

Hilton Head Island and began shipping timber from Possum Point (now Palmetto Bay Marina) to ports all over the world — Europe to Africa. In June of that year, Mother and Daddy, with their young family, moved to the Island. When I asked Mother how she felt when Daddy suggested this move, she said, "I never considered not going. I wanted to go." Mother decided and never looked back.

Sawmill on the south end of the Island.

Loading timber for shipment.

What role models Daddy and Mother provided for us! While Daddy worked from dawn till after dark in the sawmills and woods, or in later years, on Island development, he counted on Mother's looking after us and running the household. Every part of keeping house and raising a family was more complicated than it had been on the mainland. Though Mother could buy a few staples at Matilda's store on the paved road near Jenkins Island, trips to the grocery store in Savannah were infrequent and required a boat trip to the mainland. Refrigeration was limited—an *ice*box on the back porch and a rented freezer locker in Pritchardville on the road from Hilton Head Island to Savannah. An icebox actually had a large block of ice in a special compartment to cool the interior. Beneath this section was a pan, which caught water as the ice melted. Mother had to remember to empty it regularly! At first, she had to cook on a wood stove, but soon added a two-burner gas camp stove. Clothes were washed by hand and hung on a clothesline in the field beside the house. Daddy hired Louise to help with some of these tasks. Nostalgically, I say, "What an adventure!" But in truth, this life required determination, hard work, and love. And Mother was always lonely.

In addition to being a mother and homemaker, Mother served as hostess to many business associates of Daddy's who came to the Island. Since there were no restaurants, Daddy would bring these men home for dinner in the middle of the day. Sometimes he had remembered to tell Mother in advance of these visits, but sometimes Mother was taken by surprise and had to scramble to put together a meal. She could not, of course, run to a grocery store. She recorded in her diary such comments as, "We had to scratch to have a good lunch." Or, "We are sort of low on food but got along all right."

Usually, Mother fed us supper before Daddy came home from work. On those occasions, she read aloud to us as we ate. Mother loved to read, and she wanted us to love books, too. Late in her life, she once told me, "I think my greatest sin is that I like to read too much. I read when I should be doing other things." Among the books she shared were *The Adventures of Tom Sawyer*, *The Adventures of Huckleberry Finn*, *Robinson Crusoe* (which we, including Mother, thought boring), *A Tale of Two Cities*, *Great Expectations*, and most of the Miss Minerva and William Green Hill series. The first book in the series, *Miss Minerva and William Green Hill*, was written in 1909 by Frances Boyd Calhoun, who died shortly thereafter. The book was so popular that the publisher hired Emma Speed Sampson to continue the series. She wrote four more books. We didn't know about political correctness then, but rereading sections of the Miss Minerva books now, I cringe. Mother must have changed some words as she read aloud.

Another favorite book was *Punda: The Tiger Horse*, the story of a zebra in the African veld. Mother checked it out from the Savannah Public Library many times, until one day she discovered it was no longer available. The library had discarded it because it was worn out! Mother searched unsuccessfully for another copy. Apparently, the book was printed only once, in 1937. Eventually my brother Byron found one and gave it to Ginny and Kendall, our nieces. I recently reread the story and found it just as engaging as the memory—and true to my African experiences.

The best book of all was *The Swiss Family Robinson*. In 1952, when Byron was a newborn, Mother would sit in a black rocking chair in her bedroom at the back of the house as she nursed him. Rocking gently, she read to Frederick and me as we sat or sprawled on the floor near her, with our bare feet and shorts. We watched the shifting leaves in the sycamore tree, ruffled by a warm breeze which came through the window. Her voice led us into the story. I'll never forget the huge python swallowing the Robinsons' donkey! Hearing the distress cries from the poor beast, the family followed and saw the python already crushing the donkey in its thick coils—too late to rescue it. When they returned later, the children saw the serpent, lying still with the donkey-sized lump in its body.

To stay in touch with the world on the mainland, Mother constantly wrote letters. She and Nana corresponded almost daily. If no letter from her came in the mail, Mother wondered what might have happened; and there was no telephone to pick up, call, and find out. She kept up with cousins and friends in Georgia, Florida, and Virginia. In the early days, mail was delivered to the Island three times a week. The post office was located in a house at the corner of Pope Road (now Squire Pope Road) and the paved road. The postmistress, Miss Milley, lived on Honey Horn Plantation in a house near the end of the field. As Miss Milley drove her 1932 Chevrolet by our house on her way to the post office, one of us ran out to hand her Mother's letters for the day.

In the afternoon, on mail days, she stopped again to drop off the mail. The mail opened the outside world to us. A day's delivery could include *Life* magazine; a Book-of-the-Month selection for Mother; or a 78-rpm record from Children's Record Guild, a series by the American Recording Society. "A-Whaling We Will Go" brought rousing songs of life on the sea. Danny Kay sang Hans Christian Andersen tales, describing the homely duckling who developed into a swan, leading us to dream about what we could become. And we laughed aloud at the emperor's invisible new clothes! Cowboy selections like "The Chisholm Trail" led to fantasies of the Wild West. Frederick still has some of these recordings, but I've not listened to them again.

All of these stories fed our imaginations and provided ideas for playing on our own.

Getting There

Moving to the Island was not as simple as the statement. Daddy couldn't load our belongings into a truck and drive up to our new home. When the truck arrived at Buckingham Landing, outside Bluffton, South Carolina, everything had to be unloaded and transferred onto a boat for the journey to the Jenkins Island Landing, the entry to Hilton Head Island. Daddy handled this part of the move without us.

Our first family trips to Hilton Head Island were made on Charlie Simmons' *Alligator*, a boxy craft which Mother told us had once been a sailboat. Charlie made regular runs both to Buckingham Landing and to the market on River Street in Savannah, providing Islanders a link to the mainland. Our first car was brought to the Island on the roof of the *Alligator*, as were other cars and trucks. On a good tide, the trip to Buckingham took about forty-five minutes. At other times, if the captain was not careful, the boat could run aground on a muddy marsh bank, where it remained until the tide turned.

Late one evening, as our family returned from Savannah, we boarded the *Alligator* at Buckingham Landing, as usual. The tide was going out and, as the boat rounded the first buoy in the river, it stopped with a jolt. Try as they might, the crew could not budge the craft from the mud bank. There was no choice but to wait until the tide turned and rose enough to set us afloat. So we spent most of the night on the boat. The Gullah passengers took it in stride. In my memory, it seems every one of them had a pot of the most delicious-smelling shrimp and rice, but Mother didn't let us eat any of it. I can't remember if we had any sandwiches of our own, but Mother snuggled us in her arms and let us nap.

The Alligator, *docking at Jenkins Island Dock.*

The Alligator, *unloading at Jenkins Island Dock.*

    The Gullah Islanders regularly traveled to Savannah to sell their crops in the City Market. All staple supplies were brought back to the Island by boat. Charlie had trucks and delivered these necessities. To our house, he brought huge blocks of ice for the icebox and cartons of toilet paper and paper towels. The big boxes made wonderful playhouses and forts. Matilda's small general store sold the most basic necessities. Mother shopped there for bread, eggs, and a few canned goods.

Getting There

The Irene, 1950.

Charlie had other boats. The *Roly Poly* had been built as a military landing craft. The *Irene* made regular passenger runs but was too small to carry freight. I picture a white boat with orange trim. But my main memories of rides on the *Irene* are of sitting inside the small cabin at night—singing "Goodnight, Irene"!

Honey Horn had a wooden Chris Craft boat, called simply "the Chris Craft," which was used for unscheduled trips to the mainland. It was kept in the boathouse beside the Armstrongs' house. In the earliest years, when there were no telephones on the Island, Daddy went over to the mainland almost every day to make calls from Buckingham Landing, to conduct business in Savannah, or to make a trip back to Hinesville. We kept a second car at Buckingham Landing. If Nana and Grandfather, Mother's parents, or Grandmother were coming for a visit, they let us know by mail or told Daddy when he called from the mainland and someone met them in the Chris Craft at an arranged time.

In 1953, our third year on the Island, the SC Highway Department began a ferry route to Hilton Head Island. It, too, ran from Buckingham Landing to Jenkins Island, making a limited number of trips per day in the daylight hours. The first ferry was a black creosoted barge, pushed by a rectangular, stubby, yellow tugboat named *Gay Time*. Mose Hudson was the ferryboat captain. The barge was large enough to carry only four passenger cars. When a large truck was on board, it could fill half the barge. Mr. Hudson placed the vehicles according to their size and weight, directing each driver exactly where to park, then setting blocks before and behind the wheels to prevent the car from rolling around. When the ferry docked, Mr. Hudson removed the blocks and directed the cars off the barge in an order which prevented listing.

The Pocahontas, *the second ferry, 1953.*

Traffic grew so that after some months, the *Pocahontas* replaced the *Gay Time*. The *Pocahontas*, with slighted rounded sides, had been constructed as a ferry and used previously in Virginia. There was a raised bridge slightly off-center. On one side, cars had to pass under the bridge. Nine cars could fit on this ferry, individually positioned to maintain stability. By late 1955, as tourists began visiting the Island, getting onto the ferry on the weekend was harder. Often a few cars were left on the Island after the last ferry run on Sunday. In fact, a few cars were often stranded on the beach, caught by the tide.

What's in a Name?

This story began long before the move to Hilton Head Island. Daddy's father, George Byron Hack, whom I never knew, was a country doctor. Ethel Orion Davis married him when she was sixteen. Her wedding ring was a plain gold band with the date (12-19-11) inscribed inside. After Grandmother remarried years later, she gave me that ring, which became my wedding band. I'm happy Gerry was agreeable to my using this ring, because I love wearing a part of family history on my finger.

Daddy, Frederick Courtland Hack, was their first child, born February 16, 1914. In later years, as he sat before his lopsided confectioner's sugar birthday cake (which I had baked), he said, "Sometime, Valentine's Day will catch up with me." The Hacks lived in rural Walthourville, Georgia, in a house I never saw. I visualize a dirt road, an unpainted house with a screened porch, a hand pump in the yard, and children with bare feet. Two years later, Daddy's brother, Orion Davis, named for their mother, was born. Their sister, Jane Bacon, was born in 1923.

Daddy grew to be tall and gangly—a basketball player on his high school team. He graduated from Bradwell Institute in Hinesville after the eleventh grade; most schools had only eleven grades in the 1920s. When their father died in 1935, Daddy and Orion took over the management of the family's farm interests and other affairs. A few years later they added sawmills and timbering. Daddy was a whiz with numbers. With the help of a mentor, he taught himself surveying and became a licensed surveyor. For years, he was the only licensed surveyor on Hilton Head Island. In order for a new subdivision plan to be recorded, it must bear the signature of a surveyor registered in South

Carolina. There were several survey crews who prepared plats and brought them to Daddy for review and signing. His role continued into the early development of Sea Pines Plantation, when their survey crews would bring plats to Daddy for his signature.

Rheumatic fever as a child had weakened Daddy's heart, the root of a recurring cycle in midlife. He'd work until his heart gave out and he had to go to the hospital. He'd check himself out before the doctor released him, hop on an airplane, and be off to finalize another business deal. He died in January 1978, not quite sixty-four years old.

Mother, Will (Billie) Davis Stebbins, named for her mother, Willie Davis Stebbins, was born May 14, 1915, in Manatee, Florida. Her mother always regretted that she had been named "Willie," so was sure not to inflict that on her daughter. Mother's grandfather, Christopher Hartwell Davis, built bridges for the Seaboard Railroad during Florida's boom years. Her father, Charles Clayton (C. C.) Stebbins, was a banker and businessman, dealing in real estate investment.

Mother, too, had a younger brother and sister: Charles Clayton, Jr., two years younger than she, and Elizabeth (Bettie) Jane, born six years later, in 1923. Bettie told me recently that her birth certificate read "Jane Elizabeth," but since she was never called Jane, her legal name was changed. Mother grew up in Fort Lauderdale, Florida; Savannah and Brunswick, Georgia. In describing her early life to me, she said, "We moved a lot." In 1933, she entered the University of Georgia in what she described as the first class to accept women students. Because money was scarce, she did not graduate, but qualified for a teaching certificate. After teaching for a few years, she entered Georgia State College for Women (now Georgia College and State University) in Milledgeville, Georgia, where she graduated in 1939. Before marrying, Mother taught high school English, French, and Latin in Clyo, Darien, and Hinesville, Georgia. She was teaching in Hinesville when she and Daddy started courting. At that time she was boarding with General Joseph Fraser and his wife, Miss Pearl. But she took her meals with Daddy's mother, where they often saw each other. Mother told me he helped her with math problems when she was "drafted" to teach high school mathematics, "which [she] hated."

Daddy and Mother's families had "always" known each other, and even had some in-laws and cousins in common. One of Daddy's first cousins, Lucile McIntosh (Sauls), was a close childhood (and lifelong) friend of Mother's. Billie and Fred were frequently together when their families spent summers in Townsend, Eulonia, and Shellman Bluff, a riverside retreat near the coast between Hinesville and Darien. We later visited cousins at Shellman Bluff. Their cabin on the river had an outdoor shower. Though the shower was enclosed, it was exciting to me to feel I was undressed outside. Years later, on an African safari, I learned the greater joy of being able to look up at the sun or the stars—or even at animals grazing nearby. There is a sensuous joy in the warm water droplets hitting my hot skin, and soap running down my legs onto the plank floor. We now have our own version of the outdoor shower!

When I asked Mother about Daddy's proposing to her, she said, "I was completely surprised!" Nonetheless, she accepted. Daddy, on the other hand, said, "I always knew I would marry her." A typical male claim? Mother was only five feet three inches tall compared to Daddy's six foot three, but she always sat or walked with her back completely straight. She had a determination to match her bearing. I never knew Mother to hesitate to make a difficult decision, because she always knew the "right" choice to make. Maybe Daddy had recognized this early and that's one reason he always wanted to marry her.

On March 28, 1942, Fred and Billie were married in the Methodist church in Townsend, Georgia. Mother's grandfather, Christopher Davis, had built this church as a memorial to his late wife, Sarah Matilda Avary (Davis). Mother's Bride's Book lists under Our Wedding Journey "to Louisa, Virginia." Just after the

Depression and with the United States newly engaged in World War II, there was neither time nor money for a real honeymoon. Daddy had to return immediately to his work as a surveyor for the Corps of Engineers, drawing and updating topographical maps. When the war began, there was an increased need to develop such maps. I regret not asking Daddy more about the work he was doing then.

Billie and Fred Hack on their wedding day, 1942.

Mother, photographed by Daddy, 1944.

In the following years, Daddy and Mother lived mostly in Virginia, in a series of boarding houses, which suited Mother since she never liked to cook. Under "Memories" in her Bride's Book, she listed the different places where they lived. Once she wrote: "cooked first meal Sept. 12, 1942." This was five and a half months after their wedding! While Daddy worked, Mother made friends, with whom she corresponded for a lifetime; wrote letters; and read avidly, quickly finding the public library in every place they lived. For a while, she had a little pet turtle, which she staked out in a grassy yard. Daddy, in his free time, enjoyed his hobby of photography. He developed his own film, using a closet as a darkroom. We have a few of these early photos. One shows a side view of Mother with her face reflected in a mirror. It's too bad Daddy didn't take more of our family pictures. Mother consistently cut off someone's head or even half a body.

In the evenings, Mother sometimes read aloud to Daddy. One book they read together was *The Virginian* by Owen Wister. I have the copy from which Mother read to him. It was given to her by her mother, who had received it as a birthday gift in 1915, "from Mary." Mary is not further identified, but was likely her sister. Later Mother read this book aloud to us. She was impressed by how polite cowboys were and hoped we would learn from them. The unnamed Virginian first appears in the story in a bar, playing cards with a group of other cowmen. The novel's villain, Trampas, thinks the Virginian is too slow in bidding, and calls him a "son-of-a-____." To which he replies with the oft-quoted, "When you say that, SMILE." This book is considered by some to be the first serious Western novel.

By the time I was born on July 13, 1945, Mother and Daddy had returned to Georgia and were living in Townsend with her parents, Nana and Grandfather. This was Friday the thirteenth, which must have been a lucky day for all of us. I was named Martha Avary for a dear cousin of Nana's, Sallie Mat McIntosh, and for my great-grandmother, Sarah Avary Davis. Later we lived in Brunswick, then moved to Hinesville. My brother Frederick Courtland, Jr., was born October 12, 1947, Columbus Day, in Savannah. Apparently, Daddy drove through heavy rain to Townsend, where I was staying with Nana and Grandfather, to tell us of Frederick's arrival. This rain which washed over US Highway 17 was likely caused by a storm informally called Hurricane King, which hit Savannah in full fury on October 15. Completing the idea of all our birthdays being near or on significant days, Mother's periodically falls on Mother's Day.

Mother insisted we be called by our full names; nicknames were not considered. This caused difficulties from the start: "Avary" was not a name young Frederick could master. So he was allowed to call me simply "A," which somehow Mother allowed to persist throughout my life. I, and everyone else, called him "Frederick" since Daddy was "Fred." I had to contend for years with a name not spelled in the most common way and usually reserved for boys. At times I was assigned to boys' physical education classes, and once, much later, assigned a male roommate at a conference when I was in my thirties! My two namesakes have had to argue with teachers about the correct spelling of their names, too. Then there was the added complication for me of being called by my middle name. Many times, I had to answer to "Martha." The final time was when I applied for a new Georgia driver's license after Gerry and I married. The examiner was adamant I could not drop my first name, even though I showed him my new Social Security card, which had been easily changed. Finally, I prevailed. This is all part of the cost of carrying your genealogy in your name.

Another part of this genealogy is that I was born in and spent my formative years in the segregated South, before Martin Luther King, Jr., inspired us or the Civil Rights Bill of 1964 showed us the way. Nana, my maternal grandmother, was the daughter of a Confederate Army veteran. For those of her generation, the War Between the States was recent history and I heard them discuss it as such—almost as though it had just ended yesterday—or not at all. No matter whether you are on the right side or the wrong, defeat hurts. Though all my relatives, particularly my parents, were respectful of our black neighbors, neither they nor I were shocked by segregated schools, separate bathrooms for "White" and "Colored," nor even the occasional racial slur. Because I lived in those times, my awareness of the pain of our current state of relations between the races in America is deep. Most white Southerners of my generation are, to quote a friend, "recovering racists"; some degree of racial prejudice has been embedded in our souls. Given time, most of us try to be "better." We carry not only our ancestors' names.

The Lay of the Land

The original entry to Honey Horn Plantation was by a lane which turned right off the paved road, just after the road crossed Jarvis Creek. The lane ran parallel to the water, almost due south. The first structure on the right was the Big House, a long frame house, painted white. The original section of the house was built before the War Between the States, but had been expanded in the 1920s and 1930s. By the time we came, its owners were on the Island only in the fall and winter when they came to hunt. The roofs of all the houses were finished with square asbestos-cement shingles, set on the diagonal. Adjacent to the Big House was the manager's house, another rambling, white frame house. Mr. Armstrong and his wife, Margaret, and her mother, Mrs. Lawrence, were living there when we came to the Plantation. The late Mr. Lawrence had been the Plantation manager. At his death, Mr. Armstrong became manager. To the side, on the creek, was the boathouse.

The lane was also Spanish Wells Road, which from the Armstrongs' house continued away from the Plantation, straight across Meeting House Branch, and to the Jonesville and Spanish Wells neighborhoods. Almost opposite the sidewalk to the Armstrong house, a road turned off to the left and across the cattle guard into the first field. To the right, inside the cattle guard, was the house where we lived. Mr. Lawrence had built this house for his daughter Margaret and her husband, Ted, when they married. It was a spacious house with two bedrooms, one bathroom, and large screened porches on the side and back.

Just past our house and the grape arbor on the left, the road split, one lane continuing straight, the other going right toward Meeting

Key to Map of Honey Horn Plantation

1. Big House
2. Armstrongs' House
3. Boathouse
4. Our House
5. Shop
6. Taylors' House
7. Big Barn
8. Tack Room and Adjacent Buildings
9. Honey Horn Chapel
10. Dog Kennels
11. Miss Milley's House
12. Jumper Barn
13. Cattle Guard
14. Grape Arbor

Our house.

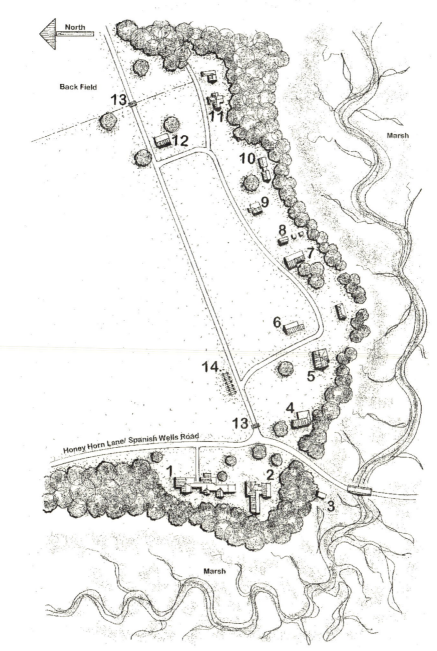

Honey Horn Plantation (map created by Hank Ross).

House Branch, which joined Jarvis Creek. Next along the creek was the Shop, which was a combination garage and workshop. At one end of the Shop, accessed by exterior doors, were the laundry room, where washing was done by hand, and the utility room, housing the diesel generators, which provided power for our electric lights. In the same room were the water pumps and tanks, as our water, of course, came from a well. In later years, we found in the garage what we called the "Old Toilet Graveyard." There were a dozen or so porcelain toilets abandoned there, more than could have come from merely replacing those in the Plantation houses. We never learned their history.

Just past the Shop was a smaller house, into which the Hinelys moved shortly after we came. Mr. Hinely had come to the Island to work at Daddy's sawmill. He and his wife had two daughters, who were considerably older than we. One of them was a spellbinding storyteller who made up chilling ghost tales. We sat around the kitchen table while she told frightening stories—and with a knife cut bread crumbs into smaller and smaller pieces.

The Hinelys didn't stay long and the Taylors moved into this house. They were the neighbors to whom we were the closest and who endured as friends over the years. Ott Taylor moved to the Island to work with Daddy in the sawmill. He brought his wife, Essie, and their daughter, Dianne. For most of these early years, Dianne, who was two years older than I, was Frederick's and my only playmate. I envied her heavy, wavy, honey-blond hair. Mine was straight and brown, and Mother kept it cut in a Buster Brown style with short bangs across my forehead. Diane had on older brother who was serving in the Army when they moved to the Island, so we seldom saw him. Once when he came home, he brought me a delicate silver filigree bracelet from Germany, where he had been stationed. Mr. Taylor was slender and quiet. After the sawmill operations ended, he continued to work with Daddy. Byron developed a close friendship with Mr. Taylor while Frederick and I were in school. Mrs. Taylor was a bustling woman

The Lay of the Land

Byron with Mr. Taylor, 1955.

who always seemed to be struggling to lose weight. Orion once joked, "She must have lost tons." The Taylors had both a washing machine and a television before we had either.

Behind the Taylors' house stood a large live oak, and behind it was a dirt-floored garage, where trucks and tractors were stored. Next along the Creek was the Big Barn, a central feature of the Plantation. Horses were a part of Honey Horn life. In 1950, there were eight or ten Plantation horses and a couple of big white mules. During the day they grazed in the fields and were stabled at night in the Big Barn. The barn, constructed of massive timbers, had thirteen stalls, a feed room, and a tack room. The once-white woodwork was now dusty and gray. Hay was stored in the large, high-ceilinged hayloft above the barn. The farmhands mowed hay in the fields, loaded it with pitchforks into the big red truck, and brought it to the barn. The truck was backed up to the front entry of the barn. A man in the truck tossed pitchforks full of hay up to another man in the loft, who collected them into haystacks. We loved to play in the hayloft—though lying in the hay was a scratchier experience than it sounds in books, where couples make cozy love nests in haystacks. This barn stood until 1963. During a thunderstorm, we children, then teenagers, were sheltering from the rain in the barn when we heard a crash and smelled smoke. Seeing smoke coming through the trapdoor leading to the hayloft, we ducked into one of the stalls. The magnificent barn was burned to the ground. Luckily, we escaped.

Frederick with the Big Barn behind, ca. 1951

Hay truck being unloaded into the Big Barn; Pinto is in the foreground.

The Lay of the Land

Next to the Big Barn were a free-standing tack room, a feed shed, and a corn crib. Beyond were a tall stack of firewood; the turkey roost, constructed of pine saplings; and the Honey Horn Chapel. Behind them were the woodshed and the dog kennels.

Miss Beatrice Milley and her brother had lived at Honey Horn for some time when we arrived, occupying the two houses beyond the chapel and the dog kennels. Earlier, Miss Milley had been the schoolteacher in the white school, but had now been appointed postmistress. She had two dogs, a large boxer and a cocker spaniel. They were noisy and rambunctious and kept us away from her yard. If we went to visit her, she could call them to hand. The dogs were always with her in her car as she drove to and from the post office. Her brother was seldom on the Island. From time to time, a small airplane would "buzz" the houses and he would land his plane in the field for a visit.

Mr. Armstrong and then Daddy always kept some white-face cows. Originally, they were free-ranging in the woods at the South End—and even on the beach. Actually, neither Mr. Armstrong nor Daddy had brought these free-ranging cows to the Island. From time to time, they had purchased cows from Islanders and driven them to the South End. A fence was built across the Island to keep them there. It was strange to be at the beach and come across cow patties—if not the cows themselves. As early development began, the cows were rounded up on horseback, herded back to Honey Horn Plantation, and corralled in the pen behind the barn. New calves were identified and branded. Older cows were dehorned in preparation for shipment to market. A pit was dug in the field for dipping them to kill ticks and other insects on their bodies. The day before the shipment, Frederick and I begged to watch the loading. Without enthusiasm and only because Daddy agreed with us, Mother got us up and dressed before sunrise to go with Daddy to the barn—while she and Byron went back to sleep. The first big truck was already backed up to the cattle chute, and we watched as the cows were herded through the chute into the trucks. Daddy kept a few, as he always liked to have cows in the fields at the Plantation.

Cows on the beach.

At the end of the field stood what was referred to as the "Jumper Barn." Now, this was a mysterious and beautiful edifice. It had only six stalls, roomier than those in the Big Barn, each of which opened both into the bricked hallway between them, and to the outside. It was newer than the Big Barn and better maintained, though I don't believe there were ever horses in it after we came to Honey Horn. Had it once housed "jumpers," fine saddlehorses? The only clue, other than the name of the barn, is shown on the painted map that hung in the hall of the Big House: painted near the location of Honey Horn Plantation are a horse and rider jumping a fence.

When Mr. Dixon came to the Island to be the lead carpenter on a 1954 addition to our house, his wife and their daughter, Bernadette, accompanied him in the move from Hinesville. Bernadette went to the one-room school with us for at least part of one year (1954–1955), and was a playmate for the short time before they, too, left the Island. The Dixons lived in the two-room apartment over the Jumper Barn. Entering the apartment, I was struck by the smell of grease, probably because Mother fried virtually nothing. Mrs. Dixon was always stitching patchwork quilts, using crackling newspaper as batting. She must have had a particularly lonesome life on Hilton Head Island.

From the Jumper Barn, the road completed the "big circle" back to the grape arbor and our house. Across a second cattle guard, there were two more fenced fields and a garden.

Pat (W. A.) Hodges was another man who came from Hinesville to work with Daddy on the surveying team in The Hilton Head Company. Mr. Pat and his wife, Miss Wilma, and their children lived in the house at the corner of Squire Pope Road, where the post office was located. At times, Miss Wilma filled in for Miss Milley and was appointed the postmistress when Miss Milley retired. Earlier, Miss Wilma was the first attendant of the fire tower located just off the paved road, not far from their house. Her lonely job was to watch for smoke indicating a fire. Having no telephone, she would wave a red handkerchief from the window so someone could spread the alert; all available men rushed to fight the fire. The Hodges children were Edward, Dennis, and Gracie. By the time they moved to the Island, the boys were in high school and too old to attend school on the Island. Gracie was in school with us, entering the first grade in 1954.

Barefoot Days

A screened porch opened from the kitchen of our Honey Horn house. During the warm months, we ate our meals on the porch, where any breeze cooled our hot bodies. We ate on a large, rectangular wooden table covered with linoleum, with multicolored speckles all over. Daddy had sawn off the corners to prevent our hitting them and being bruised. He also made a smaller, lower table for Frederick and me. Its corners, too, were angled and it was painted white, without linoleum. Daddy always used a large (quart-sized) striped glass for his iced tea. This memory must be from the days after the icebox had been replaced with a refrigerator, which ran on propane gas. For a long time, we called refrigerators "iceboxes." In addition to the table and, in the early days, the icebox, there was a large double sink which was used for washing turnip greens, cleaning fish, or washing sand from shells brought from the beach.

A loquat tree grew off the corner of the porch, inviting us into the yard, where we spent most of our time. This tree grew larger each year, spreading its shiny, green leaves the size of horses' ears, and seasonal yellow fruit. These fruits, with their large, smooth, brown seeds, were not particularly tasty, but we liked to pick and eat them. There was another loquat tree beside the Big House, where we also picked fruit. There were three sycamore trees in the yard, which were good for climbing.

Through the years, we had a succession of dogs, all of whom lived totally in the yard, which was surrounded by a woven-wire fence. Our first dog was Karo, a small blond dog, named for white Karo syrup. He came with us from Hinesville, but wasn't much of a playmate. He met an unfortunate demise when he was run over

Byron and Frederick with Barkie, 1954.

Daddy and Mother, Honey Horn Plantation, 1954.

by a dump truck bringing a load of oyster shells to replenish one of the plantation roads. Barkie was the next, and he played a more important role. He was a beautiful collie, dark gold and black with white markings. Barkie kept a close eye on Byron, making sure he didn't go too close to the creek which ran along one section of the yard. In my mind, I can see Barkie trailing Byron as he toddled along in his sagging diaper and khaki shorts. Even then, Byron had a little tummy. Frederick and I were leaner.

As spring approached, we could hardly wait for the first day Mother would let us go barefooted. Then we didn't wear shoes for the rest of the summer, although we stubbed some toes and had a problem with the stickers (sand spurs). The grassy patch between our house and the big cedar in front of the Shop was the worst threat. We had to cross this patch to reach the Taylors' house or to take letters to Miss Milley. "Just run fast across it," Mother advised. "Then none of them will stick." It seemed to me they just stuck deeper!

Daddy had his sawmill crew build a swing set and monkey bars in the backyard. There were two swings hung from a metal bar atop two sturdy, creosoted pillars. Each swing had a removable board seat, notched on the ends to fit in the bottom of a looped chain. One swing was lower to the ground than the other, for Frederick, who was smaller. We pumped our legs, swinging high until the chains became slack, but I don't recall any serious falls. There was a single bar added at the end of the swing set. On this we hung by our knees, and Mother encouraged us to learn to "skin the cat": hanging from the bar by our hands and knees, we let our knees fall forward before releasing our hands. We took some falls while learning this! The monkey bars were constructed of metal pipes. Braced on one end was a sliding board, constructed of lumber and covered with tin, which had been in our yard in Hinesville. We had to be careful of burning our legs in hot weather.

The circle around the spreading live oak behind the Taylors' house was not surfaced with oyster shells like the rest of the roads.

Instead there was a large dirt area, where we "played cars." We had little metal cars and trucks, for which we built roads, using smooth blocks as road graders. We built bridges of sticks, and mounded dirt to make tunnels. We thought we were developing subdivisions as Daddy was doing at Forest Beach and Folly Field. One day Pinto, a paint horse, penned for some reason behind the barn, jumped over the fence and landed in the middle of our carefully modeled neighborhood—or so it seemed to us. We three scared children ran into the Taylors' yard and latched the gate behind us. Pinto was as surprised as we and quickly galloped away.

On other days we were cowboys, riding our bicycles as horses. Wearing cowboy hats and gun belts, with holsters tied around our legs, we rode madly around the circular drive connecting all the plantation buildings, firing our cap pistols.

Frederick and Avary in cowboy outfits, 1950.

Sometimes, as we rode around the circle, we found Indian arrowheads among the oyster shells. In the early days, I fear some of the shells were trucked from the historic shell rings, some of which date back several thousand years. Archeologists have not yet determined the original purpose of shell rings. One of the current theories is that they mark the spots of religious feasts, where oysters were opened and eaten, and the shells were tossed into a circle around the ceremonial grounds. Occasionally, we found a piece of Indian pottery which had survived being driven over.

In shorts and barefooted, we were mighty lawmen. Sometimes we were Annie Oakley and Lofty, sometimes Hopalong Cassidy, or the Lone Ranger and Tonto. One of us had to be an outlaw. When captured, he was "locked" in our jail, a screen wire enclosed area in the back of the Shop behind the Taylors' house.

Late in the summer, the grapes on the arbor across from our house ripened. The vines on the end of the grape arbor nearest our house produced greenish-brown scuppernongs; the other end, purple muscadines, a variety of scuppernong. Both varieties are native to the southeastern United States. Three rows of poles, parallel to the road, supported the arbor about six feet above the ground. Along the middle row of poles ran a fence onto which the vines had been trained. The vines spread over both sides of the arbor, with the grape clusters hanging just out of our reach. To pick them, we rolled empty fifty-five-gallon oil drums under the arbor; balancing on the rounded sides, and rolling them down its length with our feet, we could pick and eat the grapes. The cows liked to rest in the shade under the arbor, doubtless providing wonderful, organic fertilizer! So we rolled barefooted over piles of manure. We were always a mess when we got home.

In 1954, two additional bedrooms and two bathrooms were added to our house, one for me and one for Frederick and Byron. The screened porch was converted into a dogtrot, linking the existing house to the addition. There were two skylights in the ceiling, prone to leaks. Mother was intrigued by the idea of a dogtrot, which was common in rural Southern homes. A dogtrot was originally an open, covered area between two sections of a house through which dogs could run. Ours was enclosed with casement windows at each end, which were cranked out to open. I had always loved the screened porch, particularly reading on the green-cushioned glider—but I loved having my own room. While the loss of two of the sycamore trees and the porch was sad, the building scraps from the construction became new toys. We chose pieces cut from the ends of redwood boards, which were about a foot long and made perfect river boats. With building blocks, we built corrals on them. Cowboys and Indians traveled along the rivers of the dogtrot, with their horses and dogs corralled on board in building-block pens. We used Kleenex for everything: bedrolls, saddle blankets, clothes, tents, or tarps.

I still have a collection of "little dolls" and their furniture, which provided hours of fun. Though I had a small tin dollhouse, I usually built rooms of blocks. The mother and father dolls, dressed in simple felt garments, had pliable legs which allowed them to sit—at very strange angles—on sofas and chairs. They were a little too tall for the beds and their feet hung over the footboards. The tiny baby dolls were molded of pink plastic in a semi-reclining state, so they fit into either a crib or a stroller. They also fit neatly into a little yellow-and-blue swinging hammock. The furniture was truly marvelous: drawers which opened; battery-powered lamps; tiny lidded kitchen pots, pans, and utensils. The most amazing may have been the sewing machine, which functioned just like Nana's Singer: after the top was raised, the front edge pulled forward, and the machine was lifted to a level position. Beneath was the movable foot treadle. The minute blunt needle even moved up and down. The earliest furniture pieces were colored to look like wood and upholstery. Later ones, like the dining room set, were less realistically formed of solid red plastic.

Sometimes, when Frederick was doing something else, I played with paper dolls. I had a bridal party, Grace Kelly, and a set of Colonial Williamsburg ladies and gentlemen. There was one very shapely lady, rather like the Barbies of a later generation, for whom I "designed" clothes. Outlining her on paper, I made evening gowns, sheath dresses, and bathing suits. I colored the outfits with crayons and cut them out, complete with tabs to fasten them on. I created stories and talked aloud for the paper characters. Falling in love and weddings were my favorite themes.

Each Christmas, Santa Claus brought me a new doll. Nana made clothes for my baby dolls and beautiful Madame Alexander dolls. I liked to undress and sometimes dress them. I think it was more difficult to put the clothes back on and button them. Nana and Mother both encouraged me to sew and make clothes for the dolls. My attempts were pitiful, even to my eyes, with long, uneven stitches. For the baby dolls, I mixed white shoe polish and water to make milk, which I put in their little bottles. In most photos of me as a small child, I'm clutching a doll in my hand, which surprises me—I don't remember being that attached to them.

There is one dark and painful memory. Once in a while, we were disobedient, which sometimes led Mother to switch us. This was doubly painful, because she sent us outside to cut our own switches from a *Ligustrum* bush, which she used to switch us on the back of our legs. Rarely, Daddy spanked us with his leather belt. I doubt the value of spankings or switchings—they always made me angry, to the extent I cannot remember why I was being punished. So did it change my behavior? Knowing Mother and Daddy were disappointed by my behavior had a greater effect.

Play did not end at bedtime. Mother and Daddy would tuck Frederick and me into bed, with the door cracked to the living room. We could hear the murmur of their voices as they played cribbage or Scrabble, or with another couple, bridge or canasta. Once Mother had turned our bedroom light out, Frederick and I turned on our flashlights and burrowed under the covers. Each of us had a metal ammunition box under the bed, which we now pulled out. Inside we had Kleenex, modeling clay, and pieces of three-quarter-inch aluminum tubing (I wonder where it came from!). We rolled out the clay and cut out small "cookies" with the pipes. Surely Mother and Daddy heard us whispering and giggling.

Life on the Creek

I can close my eyes and see the marsh grass waving in the water at high tide and rising from a mud bank at low. I smell the sulfur-like odor of the marsh mud, uncovered by the receding water. I hear the marsh hens' loud, descending, clacking calls and the rustling sound of the scurrying fiddlers with their single, huge, red claws raised in defense as they pop in and out of their holes. I see the bateau shifting in the gentle current. I see the great blue heron, one foot raised, still as a statue, poised above its prey in the water. I feel pain as an oyster shell buried in the sand slices into my foot—and see the bubbles rising from an oyster bank as the tide covers it.

The fragrance of marsh pluff (mud) is a distinctive smell of the Lowcountry. When I return to the Island or anywhere along the southeastern coast, and the first whiff hits my nostrils, I relax, sigh, and know I am home.

Meeting House Branch ran behind our house, embracing us. The tidal creek ran all along the back of the Plantation. It was navigable from Skull Creek to a point beside the Armstrongs' house, where the Chris Craft was kept in a boathouse. Farther along, behind our house, the water became shallower, and then there was only bare mud as the tide went out. Behind the Shop, the barn, the chapel, the kennels, and Miss Milley's, the creek was too shallow for any craft. And then it petered out entirely

The creek was our playground, as well as a wildlife sanctuary, and it provided a small view into Island life. Daddy put a weathered, gray, wooden bateau into the creek behind our house, where it was tied to a tree. We children had great freedom to adventure in the boat. Barefoot, wearing shorts and T-shirts, we

Dianne, Byron, Frederick, Avary, and Bernadette in the creek, 1955.

used poles and a paddle to navigate the shallow water. Amazingly, pictures show only Byron wearing a life preserver. A short distance out, a barbed-wire fence kept the cows and horses from wandering. Daddy told us not to go beyond the fence, even though there was a wide opening into the broader creek, where the current was swifter. As we grew older, we sometimes ventured farther—even floating under the bridge on Spanish Wells Road. This maneuver was possible only at low tide, when the water was slightly below the bridge; by flattening ourselves into the bottom of the boat, we could glide under. We had to be sure we were back home before the tide turned and rose again. The wooden bridge was constructed of large beams and timbers held together with iron spikes. The whole structure simply lay across the channel between the ends of the dirt roadbed. Once, in a storm, the bridge floated away—but someone took a boat out and towed it back, then raised it to the roadbed again. This road, running through the Plantation, was the main access to Spanish Wells. Wagons and riders on marsh tackies traveled it at all hours.

One afternoon, as we were playing in the backyard, we heard a commotion in the marsh behind the Armstrongs' house. We hurried up the road toward the bridge where we could see what was going on farther along the creek. There were several men talking loudly and working frantically with a rope and a tractor. Drawing closer, we could see they had wrapped the rope around the horns of a free-ranging Jersey cow (not one of ours), which had wandered into the marsh and became stuck in the mud near the boathouse. By hitching the rope to the tractor, her owners were able to pull her out. I'm not sure whether she survived or not.

The marsh was alive. Though we heard marsh hens (clapper rails) cackling by day—and even more at night—we seldom saw one. Daddy told us they built their nests attached to individual stems of marsh grass so they floated up and down with the tide. Fiddler crabs inhabited the mud. When the tide was out, they dug holes, flipping tiny balls of mud into a pile beside each little hole. Fiddlers made a rustling sound as they scurried about, each male with his single large red claw raised. These pincers were large enough to grab hold of a small finger and give it a nip. Sometimes, as we waded through the shallow water, minnows swam around our feet. Of course, we tried to catch them with a fishing line! We also tried to scoop up crabs, but never caught more than one or two at a time. Since this wasn't enough for a meal, we released them back into the creek.

Great blue herons, golden-footed snowy egrets, American egrets (great egrets), little blue herons, and belted kingfishers were constant visitors, fishing for minnows and fiddlers. Occasionally, an alligator crawled ashore in our area. One afternoon, we saw a large cottonmouth moccasin in the creek, just behind the house—exactly where we played. Daddy shot it and pulled it from the water for us to see; it was a broad, gray, evil-looking creature. The inside of its mouth was as white as cotton.

Once Daddy killed a huge Eastern diamondback rattler in the woods near one of the sawmills. He brought it home, stretched it out on the road, and took pictures of Frederick, Dianne, and me standing beside it. Daddy skinned the snake and tacked its six-foot-long skin on a board to dry. It was stored in the Shop for some time.

Just in the bend of the creek, behind our house, grew a magnificent live oak, whose roots wrapped around the shoreline. It leaned over the water, spreading its large limbs like comfortable arms. About six feet up, four branches forked and made a cozy nest. I have a picture of Frederick casually relaxing there, in a classic pose with his arm behind his head. When we were feeling brave, we dared each other to climb higher—sometimes this led to tears because we were afraid to climb back down. To its right, and a little way from the bank, were the weathered remains of another large tree. This, too, was good for climbing, but had no comfortable resting places. It was a pirate ship from which we attacked the fort of the big oak. A little to the left of the big tree, a lower limb of another large oak swept down toward the water. It was just the right height for us to climb into its saddle and bounce above the mud—or the water.

Dianne with the big diamondback rattler, 1951.

*Avary, Frederick, and Dianne,
with the Taylors' house behind, 1951.
The big rattlesnake is hardly visible at the bottom.*

Frederick in the oak tree behind our house, 1955.

We explored along the edge of the creek from the fairly exposed areas behind our house and the Shop building, to the more overgrown areas behind the barn, on toward Miss Milley's house, which seemed like the deep jungle to us.

Horses for Work and Play

When we came to the Island, there were few cars or trucks, as each had to be brought over by boat. Most of the Gullah natives had two means of transportation: their legs and marsh tackies. Legend has it that marsh tackies were descendants of horses left on the Island by Spanish explorers in the sixteenth century, or perhaps they swam ashore from a wrecked ship. The Spanish made port at Spanish Wells to replenish their water supply before catching the Gulf Stream for the return trip to Spain. Why would they leave horses behind?

Marsh tackies are small, spunky, and tough. Often we saw them tethered to stakes in the open, where their only nourishment was grass from fields and the marsh. The Native Islanders rode their horses, plowed with them, and hitched them to their wagons. They rode them, either bareback or with a croker sack for a saddle; a rope tied once around the neck and once around the muzzle served as a bridle. Hitching posts or rails stood in front of the post office, Matilda's store, churches, and other gathering places. Horses also pulled wooden wagons, leaving three ruts in the dirt roads: two made by the wagon wheels and one in the middle where the horse walked. Recently the Carolina Marsh Tacky, designated the South Carolina State Heritage Horse, has been certified as a separate breed of horse, considered endangered. The Carolina Marsh Tacky Association was founded in 2007 with the mission of preserving the breed.

Some of the Plantation horses as well were used to pull wagons or a plow to till the vegetable garden. One of our favorite pastimes was riding with Dempsey, who worked at the Plantation, when he collected the garbage in a wooden wagon pulled by Logan, an

Daughter of the Dawn

*The new post office with
marsh tackies and hitching post in front.*

older, plodding, black gelding. After collecting garbage at the Big House and the Armstrongs' house, he drove to ours. This garbage was not neatly contained in plastic bags: Dempsey upended the metal garbage can into the back of the wagon, adding its fragrant contents to the pile already there, surrounded by buzzing flies. He then boosted Frederick and me up beside him onto the wooden plank laid across the sides of the wagon, which served as a seat. He clucked and snapped the reins on Logan's back, and we continued to the other houses on the Plantation. Finally, Dempsey drove through the far field, through the gate beside the cattle guard, and across the paved road to the garbage dump. There, he backed the wagon up to the pit as the wagon creaked and Logan huffed and snorted. Setting the handbrake, he climbed into the bed of the wagon, and using a pitchfork and shovel, he scraped the garbage off the wagon. Our delivery often surprised a few buzzards, which is what we called black and turkey vultures.

Mother had ridden horses most of her life and Daddy had ridden to survey timber, so they naturally taught us to ride young—and we loved it. We considered the horses our friends, talking about them by name and discussing their relative merits. Among those we knew best were:

- Pinto, a round, ginger-colored paint, whom Byron usually rode
- Angeline, a chestnut marsh tacky with a large head and slightly hard mouth, whom both Mother and I liked to ride
- Rusty, a smaller, chestnut marsh tacky, whom Frederick rode. Later, Byron rode Rusty. In the late '60s, he was sold to the Sea Pines Stables.
- Robin, a tall, proud chestnut, who liked to sit down in mud puddles with a rider. Daddy liked to ride Robin.

Loving the horses entailed brushing them, knowing all about their tack, and spending time in the tack room. On the other side of the Big Barn was an area shaded by large live oak trees and surrounded on three sides by the farm buildings: the barn, the cow shed and fenced pen, the wire-sided corn crib, the feed house, and the tack room. In the center was the water trough, a large, round wooden reservoir built of narrow vertical boards and bound with a metal cable. In 1950, Mr. Armstrong kept two Jersey cows in the cow shed and pen. Dempsey milked them daily and Mother encouraged us to watch and try to learn how to milk. Dempsey sat on a low stool and, with seeming ease, pulled the udders, releasing milk with a splash into the bucket. When it was my turn, I sat on the stool

Tack room, feed storage, corn crib, and milking barn.

and grasped an udder and pulled—and nothing happened. After a second try, I gave up in frustration.

In later years, the tack room was a favorite haunt of ours. It was large, probably twelve by twenty feet. The saddles were stored around the perimeter on polished wooden saddle trees, hung on the wall. The bridles were hung on individual wooden knobs above. We learned which bridle was used for each horse—the bits varied. There were free-standing saddle racks and chests of mysterious instruments and ointments. Saddle blankets were draped over the saddle racks to dry. The room was heated by a pot-bellied wood stove, which, some years later, caused a fire, destroying this building. On the rare occasions I'm now around a horse, I inhale and remember the rich scents of this room: leather; sweaty, damp blankets; wood smoke; and saddle soap.

Before we were large enough to ride horses, Frederick had a pony, Blackie, who was kept in our yard. Mother's diaries included entries about the trouble she had catching Blackie so Frederick and I could ride, with our bare feet in the stirrups. Occasionally, Blackie escaped from the yard. Once, the mules

*Avary and Frederick on Blackie,
in the yard at Honey Horn, 1951.*

pushed over the fence and came into the yard. Blackie used the opening to amble out into the field. Catching him there was even harder! One of Frederick's early Christmas gifts was a sporty saddle blanket to use under his small Western saddle—and chaps!

When Mother and Daddy couldn't ride with us, Gunner took us, as we were too young to ride alone. He was a loose-jointed black man, whose name we thought might have come from a time he served in the Marines. We rode mostly around the fields at the Plantation. Later, Gunner took us into the neighborhood across the creek or even along the firebreaks in the surrounding woods. Byron began to ride when he was very young. He and Gunner became special friends. Gunner called Byron "Sheriff." The Gullah natives were particularly attached to Byron, because he, too, was a "native Islander."

A One-Room School

I was so excited on my first day of school. On the day after Labor Day in September 1951, Mother and Frederick walked with me as I skipped down the dusty, corduroy road and across the paved road to the schoolhouse less than half a mile. I wore a new green-and-blue plaid dress with a short bolero jacket over it, and sandals. Mother had packed my lunch in a blue-and-gray metal lunch box with a thermos for soup. Frederick had a lunch box, too, though he didn't start school for two more years. I was so proud of a paperboard pencil box. It had a tray just under the lid and a separate little drawer with a ribbon tab. Ever one for having all the proper tools for a project, I started school with sharp pencils, a ruler, and a drawing compass, befitting my rather intense personality. In those days, I was a shy, insecure girl, but very polite. I had a habit of tilting my head to the right in thought.

Mother took my hand as we walked up the eight brick steps onto the small porch, and then into the single room of the school. My eyes widened when I saw how large it was. Light came from six, tall, double-hung casement windows along the western wall and streamed in more brightly through the high windows on the east, shining on the painted wood floor and pale green walls. Mrs. Lola Merritt, the school's one teacher, seemed like the typical "old maid schoolteacher," with her tightly permed red hair and rigid demeanor. But she welcomed me in a friendly manner: "Avary, I'll be your teacher this year. We shall have fun and learn a lot. Do you want to learn to read?"

I ducked my head and whispered, "Yes, ma'am."

Mrs. Merritt took me into the cloakroom at the back of the room, where I put my lunch box on a table. Also at the back of the

Avary seated at her desk on the first day of school, 1951.

room was the wood stove, which would provide our heat in winter. Mrs. Merritt then showed me my desk, one of five of varying sizes to fit the ages of the students. Each desk chair wobbled on an oval iron base. The wooden desks stood on graceful iron braces at each end, reminding me of the stand of Nana's peddle-operated Singer sewing machine. The top slanted slightly toward the student, and beneath was a shelf for storing books—and a pencil box. Across the high side of the top was a slot for pencil and pen, and in the right corner a hole for an inkwell. Dip pens were no longer in use, but there were ink stains on my desk.

The teacher's large wooden desk stood in the front of the room. On one corner was a small, dark bell used to call us in from recess. The blackboard ran across the entire wall behind the desk. Above were tacked black cards showing each letter of the alphabet printed in white, upper and lower cases. Below these hung maps of the world and of the United States, which retracted into metal tubes. A special reward was to be asked to "beat the erasers" at the end of the school day: take the felt erasers outside and, holding them at arms' length with your eyes closed, clap them together to get the chalk dust out.

Later in the day, I learned about the iron hand pump to the left of the schoolhouse, under a tin-roofed shed. A quart jar of water always stood beside the pump handle, as the pump had to be primed each time it was used. We poured water down the pipe as we began to pump—refilling the jar with the first water pumped up. Mrs. Merritt then introduced me to the outhouse, a two-seater, down a path behind the schoolhouse. A trip to the bathroom was never pleasant; in warm weather, the odor was dreadful, and in winter, my bottom froze. Once, as I walked to the outhouse, I had to step over a glass snake (actually a legless lizard) on the path. It didn't happen then, but these snakes can break free of their tails if caught—then grow new ones. On another visit, the resident scorpion raised his bright red-orange head on the round, wooden seat cover beside me. Though we called him a scorpion, he was really a large lizard, probably a broad-headed skink.

At the end of that first day, I was so excited to take home my paperback Dick and Jane reader, *We Look and See*, with Sally and Puff, the cat, on the cover. When Daddy came home from work, I ran to him, holding my new schoolbook. "I can read!"

He sat in his chair in the living room and gathered me into his lap. "Why don't you read to me?"

So I read the first, four-page story to him:

Look
Look, look.
Oh, oh, oh.
Oh, oh.
Oh, look.

Daddy gave me a hug and said, "You did that really well!" The book is one of my treasures still.

There were five students that year: Dianne Taylor, my neighbor and playmate; Geraldine and Robert; Billy Toomer; and I. Dianne was in the third grade. Geraldine and Robert walked to school every day from Jenkins Island, and I don't remember which grades they were in—probably fourth and fifth. Since Mrs. Merritt lived that first year with the Toomers on Jarvis Creek, near where one of the Crazy Crab restaurants is now located, she and Billy came to school together. Billy was the oldest and seemed like a grown man to me. In fact, he was fourteen and in the eighth grade. Being the shy creature I am, I was really frightened by Billy's teasing. The following year, Billy had to take a boat to the Bluffton school, since there was no high school on the Island.

For daily music lessons, Mrs. Merritt arranged us in a semicircle of ladder-backed chairs around the pump organ. She taught us songs from *The Golden Book of Favorite Songs*—it's falling apart, but I still have a copy. Our five or six lusty voices and Mrs. Merritt's quavering one warbled forth. The organ had a single keyboard and one row of stops. With her feet, Mrs. Merritt furiously pumped the two large, carpeted pedals, like a bellows, to produce the notes her fingers played. She had a preference for hymns, especially spirituals. One of the first we learned was "Swing Low, Sweet Chariot," which I want sung at my funeral. Another favorite was "What a Friend We Have in Jesus." Mrs. Merritt also taught us "Flow Gently, Sweet Afton" and several Stephen Foster songs: "Old Black Joe," "My Old Kentucky Home," "Old Uncle Ned." We weren't bothered by terms describing Uncle Ned as "an old darkie." I thought then—and still think—the term was used affectionately by Mr. Foster.

While Mrs. Merritt worked with one or two students, she assigned drawings or lessons in workbooks to the rest of us. We had math, spelling, and language workbooks. Each exercise in my third-grade language workbook consisted of a short passage, followed by questions: reading comprehension, composition skills, and penmanship, all in one exercise. One story described the platypus. Though a fur-covered mammal, it has a bill like a duck. I wanted to see one. In 2013 when Gerry and I journeyed to Australia, I finally did, albeit in a zoo. The platypus was disappointingly small.

Mrs. Merritt was a friend as well as our teacher. One cold winter day, there was no oil for the heater, which had replaced the wood stove. She walked the whole school (all five of us!) to her house (she now lived on Honey Horn Lane), lit her wood stove, and conducted the school day there. By this time, Daddy had had this small concrete block house built for the schoolteacher. This residence had a living/dining room, bedroom, small kitchen, and smaller bathroom. A stoop covered the front entry step and the back door opened toward the marsh and Jarvis Creek. On another afternoon, Mrs. Merritt invited the girls to her house and gave us a lesson on making chocolate fudge. We made a mess of her kitchen, but created something that tasted good. Mrs. Merritt never forgot birthdays and made a cake for each one—even for our parents. She iced one cake for Mother with fluffy white icing and decorated it with colorful pansies dipped in wax.

In 1954, Mrs. Merritt moved to nearby Daufuskie Island to

teach in an even more remote location, where she had only one white pupil. Author Pat Conroy later put Daufuskie schooling in the spotlight in his book *The Water Is Wide*, and the movie based on it, *Conrack*. He was teaching in the colored school. By the time Mrs. Merritt left Hilton Head Island, one end of the cloakroom had been converted into a bathroom with a toilet and sink, an electric pump had been installed for the well, and a new oil furnace had replaced the wood-burning stove. We never, of course, had air conditioning.

Mrs. Merritt's successor was Aileen McGinty, who with her husband, Pete, moved to the Island in the summer of 1954. They settled into the small house on Honey Horn Lane. Mr. McGinty was a young architect, a South Carolina native, and a graduate of Clemson University. Mrs. McGinty had been born in Los Angeles and graduated from Stanford University. Pete introduced the architectural style which shaped much of the future building on the Island: natural colors, cypress roof shingles, and stained siding. Our dogtrot/bedroom addition was one of his first projects on the Island. Soon after the McGintys arrived, they acquired two Heinz 57 dogs, Soot and Sand—black and blond, as you would expect. It was big news at school when they produced puppies.

Mrs. McGinty came to the small school on Hilton Head Island as a newly graduated teacher, young and enthusiastic. There were five students that year: Gracie Hodges (first grade), Frederick (second), I (fourth), Bernadette (fifth), and Dianne Taylor (sixth). The following year was the one time I had a classmate, when a new family moved to the Island, with a boy who shared the fifth grade with me.

Mrs. McGinty expanded our school activities. She adapted stories to plays which we performed. In addition to our major annual production of *The Littlest Angel* at Christmas, I distinctly remember our performance of *Mary Poppins*. The best part was when Mary Poppins caused the entire Banks family to float around the room—which we accomplished by climbing onto the teacher's

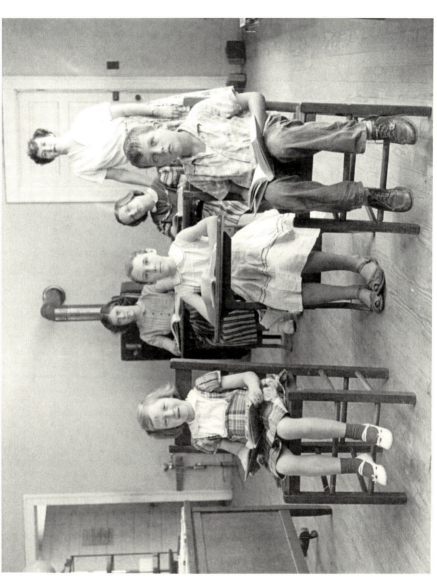

Hilton Head Island school, 1954. Left to right: Gracie, Dianne, Bernadette, Avary, Frederick; (standing) Mrs. McGinty.

desk. We also performed shorter stories from *Aesop's Fables*. In preparation, we made papier-mâché masks: fox, crow, and hare. I don't remember making a tortoise mask to accompany the hare. As Mrs. McGinty read the stories, we performed our roles.

Once a month, Mrs. McGinty went to the Savannah Public Library, where she borrowed fifty books, the basis of our classroom library. Each of us had a handmade library card to check out books.

To teach us to count money and make change, Mrs. McGinty arranged a grocery store in one corner of the room. We brought empty food cans and boxes from home, preferably with the prices on them, to stock the shelves: Eagle Brand condensed milk, Carnation evaporated milk, Campbell's Soup, Rice Krispies, and Jell-O. A customer selected items. Then the cashier totaled the prices. The customer paid and the cashier made change.

We worked together to produce a one-page school newspaper, in which we published reports on illnesses (measles and chicken pox), book reviews, drawings, and original short stories. Once I even produced a cartoon of two squirrels chasing each other around a tree. Mrs. McGinty reproduced a few copies using a mimeograph machine. She typed the stories and traced our drawings onto a thin film, which she wrapped carefully around a drum, manually coated with ink. By turning the drum, she printed copies of the newspaper. I think we sold them for five cents a copy. I have one issue of *Hilton Head School News*, apparently from mid-April 1956. In this one-page edition, Gracie had recovered from the measles and reported on the Easter Egg Hunt, and I had written a five-line book review of *Mystery in the Old Red Barn* by Helen Fuller Orton. Frederick wrote: "On April 2, Daddy, Byron and I rode over the bridge to Pinkney [*sic*] Island." The new era was almost upon us!

Though Mrs. McGinty varied our learning activities, she still drilled us on spelling, arithmetic, reading, and writing. When a student missed a word on a spelling test, she assigned the task of writing it correctly one hundred times! I sat on the front steps and wrote "Connecticut" in two columns, down both sides of a piece of notebook paper. I'll never forget how to spell it! We laboriously practiced our cursive writing on double-lined newsprint paper. I'm still not good with Qs. In third grade, the curriculum included South Carolina history. The most memorable tales were about rattlesnakes and Indians.

Our mothers helped plan a party for each holiday—and all family members came. Our preparations were artwork. For Valentine's Day, we decorated a box with red and white crepe paper, paper lace doilies, and red and pink construction-paper hearts. These were made by folding a piece of paper in half and cutting half a heart shape, freehand. Through a slit in the top of the box, we dropped our Valentines for one another—signed with question marks. Our "sweetheart messages" must be anonymous. Our mothers brought cupcakes or decorated sheet cakes and Kool-Aid for refreshments.

We regularly had art lessons. One year we made and painted clay vases. Mine was chartreuse with turquoise fish painted around

Hilton Head Island school, 1955: Frederick, Gracie, Mrs. McGinty, Dianne, Byron in front (two years old), and Avary.

it and listed to the side. Another craft we liked was making place mats. Using two sheets of construction paper, in two different colors, Mrs. McGinty cut strips—but did not cut completely to the edge of the pages. We then wove the two sheets together. Mrs. McGinty enclosed each mat in wax paper and ironed it slightly to seal it. Our parents were thrilled to receive these!

This Island school was an oddity even for our contemporaries. One day, Mr. McCracken, the superintendent of the Beaufort County Schools, brought two students over from Bluffton for a visit. My firm impression is that we were on display: children in a quaint one-room school. Maybe they had been reading *Little House on the Prairie*? Or was the purpose to show *us* some *normal* people? At recess the visitors participated in our games of jump rope, dodgeball, and red rover: "Red rover, red rover, let Mary run over!" As she ran against our clasped arms, the line broke, which was the object, and she slammed into the brick steps, getting a nasty gash on her forehead.

There is a photograph of Mrs. McGinty and her pupils taken in 1954, which has appeared many times, in history books about the Island, in magazine articles, and in museum exhibits. In the photograph, we look like bedraggled children from the farthest backwoods. Gracie is the only one of us who is smiling; Frederick's scuffed oxfords are untied; Mrs. McGinty appears to be thinking, *Just get this over with.*

Even though our school was remote, we had most of the same services as the mainland schools. Books and workbooks were provided. Many textbooks were reused year after year by the school system, but we were still thrilled to open them for the first time, as the books were "new" to us and meant we had moved to a higher grade. Oh, the smell of the occasional new book! Every six weeks, our teacher completed report cards and sent them home to be signed by a parent. In addition to academic subjects, she rated us on "deportment," twelve items including "Is courteous in speech and attitude; continues work until completed; shows pride in personal appearance; observes accepted health standards; and thinks and works independently." The only times I wasn't rated "practically always" were the first three periods in the fifth grade when Mrs. McGinty rated me "part of the time" in the last in the list! I improved thereafter.

The county nurse, Mrs. Pitts, made periodic visits to the school, when she weighed us, measured our height, and administered booster shots. One year, she gave us the Salk polio vaccine shot. Polio was a threat then, and Frederick and I had an idea what its consequences could be. We had once visited Grandmother's cousin, Arthur, who was in an iron lung. To prevent polio, afternoon naps were required. During the summer, Mother made us take a nap every afternoon—my favorite spot for a nap was the glider on the screened porch. We didn't have to sleep, but we had to lie down for an hour. It also gave her a few minutes' peace. The Sabin vaccine, which was taken as a drop of liquid on a small sugar cube, was not administered until the 1960s.

After the bridge was built in 1956, the school was closed. Billy Toomer was the first driver of the school bus from the Island to the school in Bluffton. The next year, Dianne earned her license to drive. Because Mother wanted us to go to a school where we could learn Latin, from 1956 onward, she drove us to school in Savannah every day—until another student and I were old enough to drive. Her experience as an avid reader and as a Latin teacher had convinced her of its usefulness. And Latin was a valuable part of my education; it taught me more clearly than anything else the basics of English grammar. Unfortunately, it did little for my spelling ability. When Frederick studied Latin, he and Mother read Caesar's *Gallic Wars* together with joy. As Mother's teaching led us to Latin, Daddy's engineering background strengthened our skills in arithmetic and math. In addition to helping us understand math, he drilled us on writing numbers clearly. We wrote pages of digits for him to critique. He also stressed dating any- and everything we wrote: "Before writing a word, put the date on the paper!"

The years in this one-room school with Mrs. Merritt and Mrs.

McGinty were strongly formative ones for me. Other than reading, writing, and arithmetic, the basic value I learned was always to do my best. I believe being the only one at my grade level did much to build that value, which Mother and Daddy reinforced. I never had the chance to say, "I'm doing as well as (or better than) someone else." My only benchmark was whether I had done as well as I could. Though I was always competitive in school, being at the top of the class wasn't my real goal, but doing my best. As possible proof of the quality of our early education, Dianne, Gracie, and I were all valedictorians of our high school graduating classes.

Fuskie and Dellie

When we arrived in 1950, Henry was already working at Honey Horn Plantation, and he continued to work for Daddy. On the morning after an illness put an end to his working days, Daddy went out to the Shop where the men gathered each morning and wondered aloud how he was going to get along without Henry's help. Apparently, Fuskie stepped forward and said, "Mr. Hack, you don't have to worry about that." From then on he became indispensable to Daddy—and to all of us. We loved him and he loved us.

His name was Charles Simmons #2, but most people called him Fuskie. He was a nephew of Charles Simmons Sr., "Mr. Transportation," who owned boats and provided most transportation to and from the mainland. Fuskie was born on Hilton Head Island in what is now the Lawton Stables area of Sea Pines Plantation and spent part of his childhood on Daufuskie Island, hence his name. Fuskie was a tall and dignified man, with dark skin reflecting his Sierra Leone ancestry. He always smiled and had a ready laugh. Fuskie was soft-spoken and kind. I can still feel the strong, reassuring grip of his large, but gentle hand.

Fuskie did everything to keep our lives—in fact, everything at Honey Horn—running smoothly. He chopped wood, laid fires, cut and baled hay, and managed the beef cows. He knew plumbing and could repair almost anything, from a leaking faucet to a door sagging on its hinges. He piloted the boats, washed cars, and filled their gas tanks from a hand-cranked pump near the Shop. He became the manager and supervised other workers. He could always find fresh oysters (in season), shrimp, turnip greens, or anything else, it seemed. The first seafood I enjoyed eating was raw oysters—partly because of the little cocktail forks Mother had. Daddy mixed up a cocktail sauce, dipped an oyster into it, put it on a saltine cracker, and handed it to me. I now love oysters raw or cooked, any way! Fuskie was entrusted with everything we had and every one of us. If we were away, Fuskie was left to "look in" on the house, feed the dog, and be sure all was well. If Daddy was away overnight, he asked Fuskie to come by and check on the rest of us.

Fuskie was an entrepreneur, with a number of businesses on the side. In particular, he served as caretaker for the properties of professional black doctors, lawyers, and dentists who came to Hilton Head Island and built second homes on Collier/Singleton, Bradley, and Burke beaches, then considered colored beaches. Could this business explain the collection of toilets later found in the Shop? Another business he developed was staging oyster roasts. He gained renown for his parties, roasting oysters on an outdoor fire with a large sheet of iron and wet croker sacks.

With Byron's birth in 1952, we were blessed with Dellie's joining our family, too. Louise had worked for Mother in the house since we first came to the Island, but she quickly made it clear to Mother that her job did *not* include washing diapers! So young Delphine Cohen came into our family. She either walked to work from her mother's house on Spanish Wells Road or her brother, Rufus, brought her. At some point, Fuskie started picking her up on his way to work and driving her home in the evenings. Dellie had high cheekbones and was a beautiful young woman. Romance blossomed, and in 1953, they were married.

Daddy sold them several acres of land where they built a comfortable concrete block house in the Spanish Wells community, and they lived the rest of their lives there. Delphine always had a flock of chickens and a flourishing garden behind the house, where she raised flowers and vegetables. She shared her produce generously with us and others. Unfortunately, sometimes her chickens wandered and ate snails, which was not good for the flavor of their eggs.

Dellie washed, cleaned, cooked, and took care of everything

in the house. She cooked delicious turnip greens and corn muffins, but salmon croquettes and macaroni and cheese were her specialties. At first, she washed clothes by hand in the laundry room, located in the Shop building, where she joined the women who worked at the Big House. There were deep metal sinks along one wall. A clothesline, strung in a large square, covered the area near the creek between the Shop and our house. During the hunting season, it was filled with white sheets flapping in the breeze. Flatirons were heated on a potbellied stove in the washroom, and clothes were ironed there as well. It was an uncomfortably warm room, filled with the smells of soap suds, starch, and slightly scorched cotton. Dellie and Mother were both pleased when we were able to buy a washing machine, which was installed on the back porch. I am ashamed to say the "colored" bathroom for the Plantation was in the Shop, too. There was a second bathroom on the back porch at the Big House.

Delphine taught me how to pack a suitcase when I was preparing for my trip to Europe after high school graduation. She showed me how to place the longer items across the bottom, with pants legs or the skirts of dresses hanging over the side of the suitcase. She placed carefully folded shirts on them, with their collars toward the handle of the case. After packing all items, she folded the longer items over the rest, thus avoiding creases in the pants legs and skirts. I still follow her guidelines.

Delphine was a "nanny" for Byron. When Mother began driving Frederick and me to school in Savannah in 1956, she often left four-year-old Byron at home for Dellie and Fuskie to look after. Byron spent time riding with Fuskie in his truck and "helping" with whatever tasks Fuskie was involved in that day. This was when Byron became friends with so many of the Native Islanders.

Fuskie, Delphine, and Mother became close friends. In Mother's later years, Dellie, who was also growing older, took on a new role. Byron hired someone else to do the cleaning, and Dellie came to Mother's house as an old friend who had years of shared memories with Mother. She was with Mother until her death in 1998.

A Playground for the Rich

In 1950, long before golf course communities were even dreamed of, the Big House at Honey Horn Plantation was used as a hunting lodge. During the 1930s and 1940s, Alfred Loomis and his brother-in-law, Landon Thorne, owned thousands of acres on the Island, including Honey Horn, which they used as a family retreat, as a place to entertain business associates, and for hunting. The original section of the Big House had been built before the War Between the States. To accommodate its new use, Loomis and Thorne added a wing, which included a sunroom, a large living room, two bedrooms, and two bathrooms.

According to *Tuxedo Park* by Jennet Conant, Alfred Loomis, "handsome and enormously wealthy," avoided the stock market crash and raced his own America's Cup yacht. In the early days of World War II, he quit his Wall Street career and devoted himself totally to science. According to Ms. Conant, he encouraged civilian scientists to defeat Nazi Germany and personally financed pioneering research into the radar detection systems that ultimately changed the course of World War II. Over the years, many of the guests at Honey Horn included his colleagues in banking, industry, government, and science: Dean Witter, founder of the investment company; Edward Stimson, Secretary of War; Ernest Lawrence, Nobel Prize–winning atom smasher; and even the King of Sweden—which one is not specified. Apparently, members of the famous brewing family also visited, as I have two bottles of Ballantine Burton Ale, which were part of a case of ale given to Daddy one Christmas. The label, which is rimmed by green holly with red berries, reads in part:

BREWED
ESPECIALLY
FOR
FRED HACK
ON MAY 12, 1946
BOTTLED DECEMBER 1956

Byron notes the ale was brewed for Daddy before he was known to anyone at Ballantine! Clearly, only the label had been created especially for Daddy. At one time, we had the Big House guest book signed by such luminaries; it has sadly disappeared. Photos from these days at Honey Horn Plantation show scenes reminiscent of an African safari.

As guests arrived, they settled into a world totally removed from the lives *we* lived. They selected one of the four spacious bedrooms, where fires had been kindled in the fireplaces, as they would be each morning before the sleepers woke up. Returning guests often had a favorite room. Each room was furnished with twin beds, chests of drawers, a mirrored dressing table, and paintings—some of which may have noteworthy provenance. Delicate bed linens and embroidered duvet covers adorned the beds. The ladies could request breakfast in their rooms, which was brought on wicker bed trays, spread with linen place mats. The trays were set with delicate Limoges breakfast china—a different pattern each day. And the bathrooms! Adjacent to each bedroom was a bath as large as many bedrooms. Each had a long bathtub, a sink, a toilet, a mirrored chest of drawers, a white wicker armchair, and a potbellied wood stove, also kindled early each morning. Woven cotton rugs covered the hardwood floors. In the original part of the house, bathrooms were obviously later additions, tacked onto the external walls of the bedrooms.

Running such an establishment required staff. While a number of maids and other workers were hired locally for the hunting season, there were also some permanent employees. In 1950, when my family moved to Honey Horn, Mr. Armstrong was the

Plantation manager and lived in the house next to the Big House. Albert Kemsley, an Englishman, was the chef. He and his wife lived in the Big House year-round, in rooms behind the kitchen. Mrs. Kemsley was an invalid who stayed mostly in her room. Mr. Kemsley had wavy white hair and a dapper mustache. He was short and plump—as a chef should be. The kitchen always smelled of sage, which had seasoned some quail, duck, or turkey being roasted in the oven of the cast-iron wood stove. This stove is still in the kitchen of the Big House, because it is, frankly, too heavy and large to move. In a pantry off the back porch was a trap door leading down into a wine cellar. We found no wine, but there was a wine press—for making wine from the local scuppernongs?

Curtis Thompson owned and trained the hunting dogs. He spent the summers in North Carolina and came to Honey Horn Plantation for the winter hunting season. He and his wife, Miss Julia, lived in a three-room wing on the back of the Armstrongs' house.

Once, Miss Julia had a frightening accident. Mrs. Taylor had a washing machine (before we did). The white enameled machine consisted of a large, round tub on wheeled legs, so it could be rolled from the pantry into the kitchen. A hose attached to the sink faucet was used to fill the machine for washing, with an electric agitator. The operator manually emptied the tub of sudsy water and refilled it for rinsing. The wringer was attached at the top on an arm; swinging it over the tub, the operator ran each piece of laundry through the wringer as excess water fell into the tub. The wringer consisted of two electrically powered tubes, turning in different directions, which pulled the clothing through. One morning when Miss Julia was using the machine in Mrs. Taylor's kitchen, she caught her hand in the wringer. As she struggled and shouted for help, her arm, up to the elbow, was pulled through. Mrs. Taylor came running into the kitchen and managed to disengage the wringers and free the arm. Dianne ran quickly to find Mr. Thompson and Mr. Armstrong, who took Miss Julia across the river by boat to Bluffton to see Dr. Lee. No bones were broken, but her badly abraded arm was not a pretty sight.

Mr. Thompson drove a red 1940s Chevrolet truck, with a kind of removable fence around the flatbed. The yellow wooden dog boxes were loaded onto the bed. His Hilton Head Island assistant was Jim Cohen, a black man, who knew the birds and dogs as well as Mr. Thompson. Sometimes they split the hunters into two parties and each led one into the field. In fact, Jim Cohen was the first in a family of dog trainers: his son and grandson followed in his footsteps, training coon dogs for people all around South Carolina.

The Hunt

Early on a winter morning, as I lay in bed, I could hear the rattle of the cattle guard as a truck crossed and stopped in front of our house. Then came the murmur of men's voices, a laugh, as greetings were exchanged. Shortly, there followed the sounds of horses' hooves, the creaking of saddle leather, and the jingle of bits and harnesses as Henry brought the horses from the barn. He spoke softly with the others, bent down from his saddle, opened the gate beside the cattle guard, and rode off at a trot down the road, leading the horses. This was the beginning of the hunt.

On hunting days, the dogs and horses were assembled in front of our house. Henry, or later Gunner, rode ahead with the horses to the selected hunting area. A few of the hunters rode English saddles, but most of the saddles used were US Army McClellans, which were open through the middle of the seat. Shotgun scabbards hung from the saddles with saddlebags buckled on behind for extra cartridges. Hunting locations varied from fields and the Big Woods in the area which is now Hilton Head Plantation, to more distant locations at the South End, now Sea Pines Plantation. In the early days, Loomis and Thorne hired Mose Hudson, who was later the ferryboat captain, to ride on horseback through the woods patrolling for trespassing poachers. He was also responsible for ensuring the area was well stocked with game.

The hunters rode with Mr. Thompson in his truck or with Mr.

Armstrong in his black Chevrolet coupé to meet up with the horses at the hunting location. Both men and women participated. Some of the hunters were stylishly dressed in jodhpurs, long polished leather boots, and tweed shooting jackets. Other parties wore khaki pants and plaid flannel shirts. Usually they hunted quail, turkey, or ducks. Occasionally, an evening dove shoot was arranged.

Hunting operations continued into the late 1950s, even after Daddy assumed management of the Plantation. Daddy sometimes joined the hunters in the field. We children, of course, never did. But once or twice we watched Mr. Thompson work the dogs. He released several pointers into a field. They circled excitedly until they caught a scent. Cautiously they stalked the covey of quail to their hiding place among tall clumps of grass, where the dogs assumed "the point" to locate them for the handler. The hunters dismounted and approached, walking slowly toward the best vantage point for a shot. With a sudden rush of wings beating fast, the birds flew into the air; a volley was fired. Usually, there were birds for the dogs to retrieve. These were pocketed and later stacked on the back of the truck. The precision of the working dogs was beautiful to see.

Though fowl was the primary game, sometimes a deer drive was arranged, which was quite different. Each hunter was led to a stand. This wasn't a constructed and raised stand, but an assigned spot in the woods, where the hunter was to *stand* and wait for the deer to pass by. Then men on horseback rode through the woods with deerhounds and drove deer toward the stands. Staying on one's stand was crucial: a wandering hunter could be mistaken for a deer. One Thanksgiving, there was an accident. Byron and Frederick participated in this hunt with Daddy and were assigned their own stands. As a deer appeared before him, Byron shot, but missed the deer. Daddy walked out of the woods and said to Byron, "Son, I think you've shot me in the leg." Daddy rightly took the responsibility for the accident: "I shouldn't have left my stand." In the excitement, no one remembered to cut

Byron's shirttail because he had missed the shot. Daddy's wound wasn't serious.

I remember the day Frederick killed his first deer. He strode into the house with blood on his face as well as a proud smile. As was the tradition—and I think it is still followed—some of the blood of that first kill is smeared on the hunter's face.

Mr. Thompson had both long-haired setters and short-haired pointers, which were kept in the kennels, beyond and behind the chapel. Six fenced runs, each about ten by twelve feet, opened into rooms in a long building. Several dogs shared each run. Beside the gate to each was a water faucet, where the two-quart aluminum pans in which food and water were served could be cleaned. Dempsey prepared food for the dogs in a small dog kitchen. Cornbread and turnip greens were added to Purina dog chow, which Dempsey cooked all together in a large iron pot mounted in the kitchen. Another nostalgic smell—warm and wholesome.

In the same area, we watched as game was skinned and cleaned. Decapitated turkeys and ducks were hung from a line for the blood to drain. Quail were too small for this treatment and were laid in stacks on the edge of a table with the blood dripping down. Deer were hung by their hind legs from a tree limb for skinning and cleaning. This process naturally caused an uproar of barking from the dogs, who were usually rewarded with some meat scraps at supper. After cleaning, the meat was butchered and hung in the "smokehouse" for aging and curing. This was a small (six by six feet) screened enclosure near the back porch of the Big House. Actually, no smoke was involved. The kitchen staff later sliced the meat into the proper sizes for cooking on a wooden table on the back porch—which Gerry and I still have on our porch, marked along the edges by the knives and cleavers.

Hunters posing after a turkey hunt behind Mr. Thompson's truck, grape arbor is behind, 1951.

Daddy after a turkey hunt, with the Armstrongs' house behind, 1952.

After the Hunt

The hunters returned to the assembly area in front of our house, where we sometimes watched as they posed for pictures, with the turkeys they had shot hanging from the back of the truck or held in their fists. They walked the short distance back to the Big House, stored their guns in the gun room, and shared tales of the morning "safari" around a crackling fire in the living room. As they walked down the hall to the living room, they stopped to look at a hand-painted map of Hilton Head Island. The four-by-seven-and-one-half-foot masterpiece named the various nineteenth-century plantations, highlighting features of each area: a small praise house, a flying duck, deer, flushed quail. The painting is signed by Gerald Brian Doe, who dated his creation 1939.

There were other intriguing paintings in the house as well, which the Thornes and Loomises had brought by yacht from their homes on Long Island. Among my favorites are two fanciful egrets, collages "painted" in colored feathers. Several early Audubon bird prints and framed newspaper etchings illustrating Island battles during the War Between the States hung on other walls. The gracious living room was huge, with several seating areas. There were a long, cushioned sofa and wing chairs beside the six-foot fireplace, over which hung a large, round, gilded eagle mirror. A couple of game tables with chairs were set in the corners, and a library table was placed in front of the large bookcase, which covered an entire wall beside the fireplace. Among Mother's treasures, Byron found a typed note, now lost, saying the living room at Honey Horn was a duplicate of one in a Long Island house.

After warm baths, the guests, dressed in fresh clothes, assembled for dinner before the fireplace in the dining room. Photographs show them wearing not tails and evening dresses, but comfortable country attire. The table was covered with a crisp linen tablecloth and laid with heavy English silver-plated flatware and a set of hand-tinted Lowestoft Deer blue-and-white china. The Lowestoft Deer china was manufactured by Booths in England. Mother's research led her to believe the standard blue-and-white pattern had been tinted by hand as a special order. The orange-and-green tinting certainly differs from piece to piece. Glassware glittered in the light from the overhead chandelier. Chef Kemsley would have prepared some game from the prior days' hunts. Maids in white uniforms and caps served the meal from the butler's pantry, located between the kitchen and the dining room. And so a hunting day at Honey Horn Plantation ended.

Kinfolks and Wild Birds

When people came to visit us, they had first to arrange for a boat to bring them from the mainland, so it was rare for anyone to just drop in. Most of our visitors were family. Nana, Grandfather, Mother's parents, and Grandmother, Daddy's mother, were the most frequent. When Nana came, she usually brought new clothes she had made for us, mostly for me. Grandmother brought delicious pound cakes and yeast rolls she had made.

Daddy's brother Orion was frequently with us at Honey Horn. He slept in the dining room on a rollaway bed, which had a severe dip in its middle. Orion was tall like Daddy and a handsome young bachelor. His was smart and always into a new project. He was probably the first residential real estate agent on the Island. Orion was an environmentalist and naturalist, and developed a new hybrid of hibiscus, which he called the Hilton Head Island Hibiscus. He crossed a "Painted Lady" with a wild Island hibiscus to create a plant with a deep red bloom. When Folly Field was developed, Orion bought one of the first houses and moved to the Island in 1953. Grandmother and her second husband, Wallace F. Martin, and Nana and Grandfather also bought cottages there, on the front row. When an unusual tornado struck, only their two houses were destroyed.

Orion also liked to cook, so he and Mother concocted some strange foods. They made brunswick stew using squirrel meat. Once, he and Mother decided to make hogshead cheese. I don't remember if it was a success, but do I remember the hog's head resting on the drain board of the back porch sink. Orion loved to travel to Mexico, where he would meet Sam, his special guide and friend, at the border. After one trip, Orion acquired Chita, a Mexican Chihuahua—the first in a succession of yippy little dogs.

From the beginning, Orion was a major influence in our young lives. He and Daddy taught us to play poker so we couldn't be "taken advantage of." And where would that have occurred? At this point, I was the barefoot girl in rolled-up blue jeans, with a shirt tied at the waist. But Orion assured this withdrawn and painfully shy niece she was pretty; that boys, who actually had no clue I was alive, were flirting with me; and I should be proud of myself. "Just be sure to keep a straight part in your hair." From a dashing bachelor, these words carried weight. And Mother always added to this, "Sit up straight and don't frown. It will give you wrinkles."

Daddy's sister, Jane, and her two daughters, Janet and Meg, visited less frequently, coming with Grandmother. Jane had married Lloyd Allen, whom she met when he was in the Army at Fort Stewart during the war, and they had moved to Harlingen, Texas. Occasionally, when they were with us, Lloyd flew his plane over, buzzed the house, and Daddy picked him up at the air strip—a grass field in what is now Port Royal Plantation.

Mother's brother, Charles, came sometimes. He helped Daddy with legal matters as The Hilton Head Company developed. After Grandfather and Nana bought the cottage at Folly Field, he occasionally brought his family. Mother's sister, Bettie, who also visited us, seemed to me the female counterpart to Orion. I used to fantasize that they would marry. She was single and wore clothes with more vivid color and, to me, more style than Mother's—and red polish on her fingernails! I particularly coveted a pair of red, high-heeled pumps she wore. I would slip into her room and try them on. On her dresser, she kept a small collection of cosmetics: Pond's face cream, powder, rouge, and eyebrow pencil. These items struck me as quite exotic since Mother used nothing but lipstick and Jergens lotion—maybe a dab of Johnson's baby powder on her nose. To add to her glamour in my eyes, she had a small red birthmark on her chin, which she

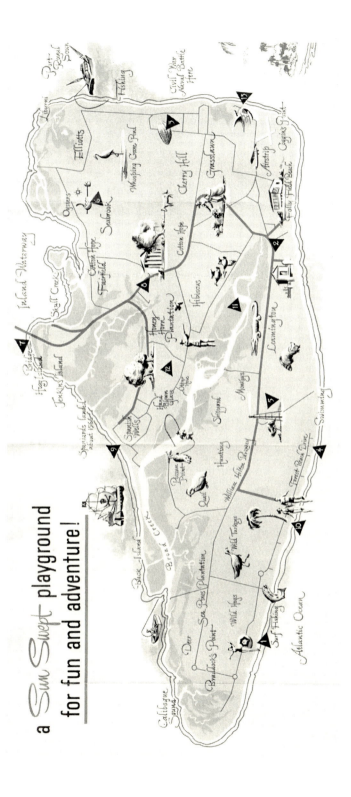

Map of Hilton Head Island, ca. 1960.
(2) Baynard Mausoleum; (5) Hilton Head Island Lighthouse; (13) Steam Guns

hated. To me it was like a natural beauty patch and I wanted one like it. Later Bettie brought her girlfriends to Nana's cottage at Folly Field. Their two-piece bathing suits, beautiful sandals, and smart sundresses made me want to grow up quickly and wear the same.

When visitors came, the main entertainment was "riding around the Island." Daddy loved conducting these tours, proudly pointing out what was going on. We would ride through the Big Woods (now Hilton Head Plantation) to spot whatever wildlife was afoot. Wild azaleas grew near the sandy roads, and we might spot white-tailed deer dashing into the woods. There were a couple of rookeries on the Island, where herons, egrets, ibis, and other water birds nested in colonies. Though these areas weren't readily approachable by car, sometimes we saw herons and egrets flying in and out.

In fields where horses or cows grazed, we sometimes saw cattle egrets. These birds were new to North America and not even included in our 1946 field guide. They had existed only in Africa until the late nineteenth century, when they first appeared in South America. We learned about cattle egrets from Virginia Holmgren, who was an experienced birder. Mrs. Holmgren told us cattle egrets had recently migrated into Florida and were moving up the eastern coast. She and her husband had lived and worked in South America before coming to the Island. Mr. Holmgren was a contractor for a mining company, searching for uranium deposits. Daddy purchased a Geiger counter and we joined him as he waved its wand over every dark patch of sand to see if it was radioactive.

On one memorable occasion, Daddy took us children into Whooping Crane Pond by boat. In preparation, he had each of us prepare an index card listing birds we could expect to see, with a brief description of each species. Fuskie and Daddy had brought the bateau from the creek to the pond in the bed of a pickup truck. They dragged it through the dense growth at the edge of the pond into the more open area. From the water, covered with green duckweed and darker water buttercup, gray-barked gum trees grew, shutting out the sun except for small golden patches here and there. The boat pushed the green carpet aside into ripples which came together behind, completely hiding our path as we wound between trees, spotted with fluffy white egrets. Other darker birds perched in the trees as well: water turkeys (anhingas) with their snakelike necks and turkey tails; Louisiana herons (tricolor herons) with white breasts and plumed crests; black-crowned night herons, white with black-capped heads and dark backs. Everywhere, high and low, hidden or in small leafless trees in the open, were nests. The bluish-green eggs, usually three of them, had been temporarily abandoned by the frightened birds in the nests made of rough gray twigs.

In the earliest days, our Island tour included the sawmill, where we could watch the men at work. Sometimes a man would be driving a skidder, pulling logs from the woods; or trucks filled with logs were dumping them into piles at the mill. We watched the lumberjacks feed sections of tree trunks through the whirring saws, with the sawdust taken by conveyor belts to the top of the sawdust pile. As one side of the log was trimmed, the men flipped it and ran it back by the saw, until all four sides were flat. The slabs, covered with pine bark, that were trimmed from the logs provided siding for temporary buildings. Alligators swam with only their eyes and noses visible above the water in the ponds where the sawmill workers bathed. On one exciting afternoon, we spotted a large alligator with a full-grown wild hog in its mouth. Daddy estimated the hog may have weighed forty pounds.

Along the way, Daddy pointed out where various Native Islanders lived. He particularly enjoyed commenting when we drove past one two-storied house along the paved road, "George Washington slept there . . . last night." George was a tall, muscular man who worked at the sawmill. Daddy said George Washington was a canny and kindhearted fellow, aware of his strength. "I saw him working with Raymond once, who was a smaller, slow-moving man. They needed to lift a heavy log, so George had Raymond take the heavy end, then he started at the light end and moved up the log until he thought Raymond was lifting as much as he should."

North Forest Beach lot sign, ca. 1956.

When development began, Daddy showed off new roads being built and lots being surveyed and laid out at Forest Beach. Daddy proudly pointed out the new signs indicating lot numbers, their sizes, and their prices. Gerry and I have on our wall one sign for a second row lot advertising the staggering price of $1,900.

As a treat at the end of one of these drives, we might stop by Matilda's store near Jenkins Island and buy chocolate ice-milk bars. In summer, they melted more quickly than we could eat them. To try to keep the drips out of the car, we put our arms out of the windows, so drips fell outside. That only made them melt faster!

Sand, Shells, and a Wolf

Mother wasn't a beach person: "I don't like the sand getting into everything." She meant shoes, bathing suits, sandwiches! We didn't live at the beach, but Mother occasionally took us to the beach to play in the waves and sand, or in cooler weather, for a picnic. Mother packed weenies and buns or egg salad sandwiches into the large brown wicker picnic basket, with paper plates, napkins, ketchup, and a jar of iced tea, and we set off for one of several beaches.

There were no houses along the Island's entire thirteen-mile beachfront. We could walk from the Old Fort (Port Royal Plantation) to Forest Beach—or even all the way to the south end of the Island—without seeing anyone. In order to walk the entire distance, one had to find a safe way to cross Folly Creek, which ran into the ocean just south of Folly Field. Several times, as a preteen, I walked alone along the deserted beach from the Old Fort to Folly Field. There, only, I was uninhibited and could sing, shout, dance, write in the hard sand—and no one knew what I did. Everything was covered and washed away by the crashing waves of the incoming tide.

We picnicked at Elliott Beach, now a part of Hilton Head Plantation. One of the earliest brochures put together to promote Hilton Head Island featured on its cover a graceful fallen driftwood tree, the principal feature of this beach on Skull Creek near Port Royal Sound. Against this windbreak, Daddy built a fire to roast weenies and marshmallows. Most of the weenies fell into the sand and we burned the marshmallows to a crisp. I still prefer my marshmallows to burst into flame before I blow out the flame and eat them, even if they burn my lips.

Avary at Elliott Beach, 1952.

Walking on Elliott Beach, we found delicate oyster shells, rubbed thin and silvery by years of washing over the sand. Many had holes worn in them, making them perfect for Mother to string into necklaces. Frederick and I made them as well, of course! Sometimes we used the natural shells, sometimes we painted them with nail polish or leftover green house paint. (Every room in our house was painted some shade of that 1950s green.) Mother and Daddy collected driftwood in interesting shapes. Daddy claimed one particular piece was shaped like the Island. Frederick, who has it still in his office, says, "It's more the inverse of the Island, revealing the perverse aspect of Daddy's character." Hilton Head Island is shaped somewhat like a shoe, broad at the northern (right) end and pointed at the southern (left) end. This piece of twisted driftwood is pointed at the right end and broad on the left. Daddy's engineer's mind had seen the reversed similarity.

Another section of the beach we visited was near the Old Fort, now in Port Royal Plantation. The name probably came from earthwork forts built on the site during the War Between the States. The remains of two steam-gun emplacements, built of heavy reinforced concrete during the Spanish American War, still stood on the beach. The best-preserved one was nestled into the headland. It had a round, rotating gun base, with compass points marked on a large bronze dial. A loaf-shaped bunker extended on either side. One of these had completely collapsed. The other had a large hole broken into the end. The second emplacement was farther out on the beach; only a few large pieces of concrete were visible. Daddy pointed across the Sound as he told us one test shot had been fired from the main gun, which set the woods afire on Bay Point across the way. The guns had been removed after the War and the site abandoned. My recollection does not fully agree with historical research, which records only one steam-gun emplacement. This is, however, *my* recollection—perhaps Island legend.

Just north of the steam gun, Fish Haul Creek ran into Port Royal Sound. We walked barefoot along the beach on the damp, firm sand to a spot where we crabbed, using coarse strings wound around short sticks. To the loose end, we tied chicken necks, apparently the preferred food of crabs. We lowered the bait into the shallow water and waited until we felt or saw a crab nibbling at the bait. We then tried to scoop the crab from the water using a long-handled net, longer than we were tall. If one escaped the net onto the sand, we ran to save our bare feet from its menacing claws. Once a crab caught my heel in its claw, which caused a badly infected sore. Mother had me soak it in warm water with boric acid. At the Old Fort we usually caught enough crabs for a meal. After we got home, Daddy dropped them alive into boiling water, where for a short time we heard them scrabbling against the top of the blue enamel pot as we almost cried. Mother explained, "This is just the way you have to cook crabs." When we sat down to eat, the meat never seemed quite worth the effort of picking it out of the shells. Now I adore crab cakes.

The beach at the Old Fort changed constantly. At times, the concrete emplacements were almost buried in sand; on another day, the water lapped against the main one and completely surrounded the smaller one. Low tide often exposed black mud banks on the beach, which looked like porous volcanic rock. In the mud crevices, we found old colored glass bottles, uniform buttons, broken china, and minié balls, primarily from the time of the War Between the States. After taking Hilton Head Island, the Yankees established a town on this headland, where for a short time, about thirty thousand people lived. Confederate Fort Walker, manually constructed earthworks, has long since washed into the Sound. Fort Sherman, another earthen fort which still stands within Port Royal Plantation, was built by Union forces as part of the blockade of Southern ports. Our uncle Orion established an arboretum among the earthworks, for which he selected plants native to the Island. He chose this location because it included various types of habitat from dry, sandy areas to wetlands. The arboretum still exists, maintained by volunteers.

Publicity photo showing beach with slew; Byron and Mother are in the foreground.

In the earliest days, Daddy built a canvas-covered shed on the beach at the end of Pope Avenue, where Forest Beach is now located. Mother and Mrs. Hinely, our neighbor before the Taylors arrived, packed a picnic and Mother drove the two families in the

Jeep to this shelter nestled into the dunes among the sea oats. Shortly after the pavement ended at the lighthouse, we turned onto Pope Avenue, which ran absolutely straight to the beach. Each of the original Island plantations on the Atlantic Ocean side of the Island had a road running directly to the ocean. On trips to the beach, the Jeep frequently rolled over a rattlesnake or copperhead sunning in the road. When Mother was driving, we went right on. But if Daddy was driving, he had to kill it. Sometimes he shot it with the white rifle he always had in the trunk of his car, but at others he broke its back by riding back and forth over it, slamming on the brakes while it was beneath the back tire. I didn't like to see the snake killed in such a bloody, gruesome way.

This shed on the beach figures in a vivid recurring dream of mine in which a large gray wolf in a short, red jacket walks on his hind legs into the shelter. It wasn't a nightmare, but rather just a story. My imagination may have been fed by Little Red Riding Hood or another fairy tale. Whenever I remember the shelter, I see that wolf!

On this part of the beach, the currents and ebbing tides left behind deep slews in which we could play, little ponds warmed by the sun—with no waves breaking in our faces. In the slews, minnows swam around our ankles and nibbled gently at our toes, while small, hermit-crab-inhabited conches, little snails, and large horseshoe crabs crawled on the bottom—or buried themselves in the sand. Nearby, we would sit on the beach and build sand castles. First, we would pack sand into our little buckets and empty the cones in a circle. As we dug a moat around the castle, water seeped into it. Mother would help us take handfuls of wet sand and carefully drip it over the plain forms to create spires or towers with window openings in them. If we built with too much water in the sand or built the turrets too high, they would crumble. While we picnicked, we had to watch the tide take our castles away.

We found more shells on this Atlantic beach than on the others: large conch shells, sailors' ears, babies' ears, angel wings, abalones, cockle shells of all sizes, tiny bright butterflies' wings, and corkscrews. If I held a conch up to my ear and closed my eyes, I heard the soothing sound of waves crashing gently against the beach and receding into the ocean, almost like breathing. Mother created a fish on a square of plywood, using small shells for its scales. Other treasures also washed ashore: plastic floats from shrimp nets, orange, white, blue; coconuts, some still edible; flat, white lifesaving rings with ships' names painted on them; barnacle-covered planks.

Daddy and Mr. Hinely joined us when they finished their day's work. They waded into the surf to fish for bass. At home, after Daddy cleaned the fish, Mother would bake them in the oven, smothered with tomato catsup. In the spring, we sometimes stayed on the beach until the moon rose, making a sparkling trail over the water. As the waves of the ebbing tide rolled gently to the shore, we watched loggerhead sea turtles make their slow way back to the ocean, after laying their rubbery eggs in nests dug near the dunes. We stood on their backs as they labored on that journey. The turtles' shells felt rough with barnacles to our bare feet; as we looked down we saw the large flippers moving slowly to drag the exhausted mother back into the water. Daddy and the sawmill crew liked to eat turtle eggs, which *could not* be cooked solid. I regret riding on these poor turtles, which are now protected under federal law.

We always took shells home with us, sometimes with the hermit crabs still inside. Dead and decaying sea life did not smell good. Soaking them in bleach helped, but it took the color out, leaving the shells dull gray. Mother would say, "Look at all this sand you have brought onto the porch!"

Let's Take a Ride

Sometimes, we visited our grandparents—usually both families in one trip. Visits with Grandmother in Hinesville were often for a meal, but we didn't spend the night. Maybe this was because her house was smaller, or maybe a habit of many young families of spending more time with the wife's family than with the husband's. I think this led us to feel less close to Grandmother than to Nana and Grandfather. Grandmother was tall and stately, and I remember always feeling the stiffness of her corset when I hugged her, which made me feel she, herself, was stiff. Grandmother was a strong woman, with iron-gray hair, who had firm control over her family. During the Second World War, already a widow, she had been a leader in the local American Red Cross. These visits to Hinesville always included a ride to Hacks Pasture to check on things.

After a visit with Grandmother, we drove on to Darien, where Nana and Grandfather lived on the Ridge, a community of homes along the Cow Horn Road (GA-99) just outside town. After Mother and Daddy were married, Nana and Grandfather had moved from Townsend into the two-story house called Magnolia Hall, built in the mid-nineteenth century in the classic Southern style. Most of the houses on the Ridge were similar in style. Wide halls ran from front to back on both floors, flanked by rooms with fourteen-foot ceilings. Every room had a fireplace—but none had closets. The two bathrooms had clearly been added more recently, tacked on to the ends of the halls. Tall, triple-hung windows opened onto the front porches, upstairs and down. The two lower frames could be raised, making "doors" onto the front porches. Short, two-panel doors covered the lower portion of each window. Was this for privacy from

*Grandfather and Nana
with Avary and Frederick, ca. 1949.*

*Grandmother
with Avary and Frederick, ca. 1949.*

the porch or to prevent someone from walking into the glass? A former butler's pantry had been converted into a galley kitchen, replacing the original detached one behind the house. After Nana and Grandfather died, the house at the Ridge was sold and later completely destroyed by fire.

At bedtime, Mother settled us into bed in what was called "Billie's room," though she had never lived in this house. Nana and Grandfather's room was beside it, with a connecting door. Every door had a hinged, glass transom above it to allow air circulation. Mother or Nana would tell us a story. Nana was short, pretty, and plump (as she had been from girlhood). From my earliest memory, her hair was white. I don't recall her ever saying anything harsh about anyone. She always managed to smile, even when she was suffering from recurring migraine headaches.

Nana knew wonderful stories about "The Tin Soldier," "Hidgy Hodgy," and "Little One-Eye, Two-Eye, and Three-Eye." I have managed to collect a few of these from older relatives and fairy-tale books. After the adults went back downstairs, Frederick and I were scared to be left upstairs. I think we were afraid of being left alone in the house, though such a thing had never happened to us. So we crept down the stairs to a point where we could hear voices. Shortly, someone would realize we were there and send us back to bed. Eventually, we fell asleep.

When we came down for breakfast, Grandfather was seated at the head of the table in the dining room, dressed in a white shirt and tie. I never saw him dressed otherwise. He was a distinguished-looking man of more than average height who wore wire-rimmed glasses. After breakfast, Grandfather would say, "Let's drive down to Blue 'n Hall." We all climbed into his big Oldsmobile and he slowly drove the short distance up the Cow Horn Road to the turnoff for Blue 'n Hall. All we saw there was a dock on the Intracoastal Waterway. Looking across we saw Hird Island, where Grandfather kept some cattle. He pointed out three small "ballast piles," small islands created where ships had unloaded their rock ballast before being loaded with coastal cotton, timber, or naval stores for the eastbound trip. Grandfather explained to us that the ballast had kept the ships' hulls deep enough in the water to not be capsized by heavy seas.

In the quiet afternoons, Nana entertained us in rockers on the front porch, where the fragrance of magnolias surrounded us. At one end of the porch, a wisteria vine grew from a magnolia tree to the porch. It was as large around as a man's thigh, and we could easily crawl along it and into the tree. Sometimes Nana told stories; at others she challenged us to count the cars that passed. Not many traveled the Cow Horn Road. As we rocked, Nana passed along bits of wisdom. "If wishes were horses, all beggars would ride." And if we complained we didn't have time for something: "Everybody has the same twenty-four hours every day; what you do with them is up to you." At four o'clock, she rewarded us with Co' Cola and half a Mounds bar. Mounds were a special treat which we enjoyed only at Nana's. Occasionally, she gave us *one* coffee-flavored hard candy.

Nana and Grandfather also had treasures on the built-in bookshelves in the living room: a set of Compton's Pictured Encyclopedias, *Saturday Evening Post* magazines, and a few toys. One of the most fascinating was a tiny iron stove, with an oven that opened. As I became a preteen, I devoured the romantic stories in the *Saturday Evening Post*, which seemed very risqué to me. In the center of each volume of Nana's 1922 edition of Compton's was a story from a series, "Tales the Woodman Told." This Woodman was "Wondrous Wise" and told his stories to a "Little Boy." They are charmingly illustrated by Hazel Frazee. We all loved it when Nana read these stories to us. My brother Byron still has this set of encyclopedias.

The journey home through Savannah along Highway 17 crossed the Ogeechee River. In the spring, Daddy stopped at a filling station near the river to buy shad roe: fish eggs! It was a delicacy he enjoyed, sautéed whole and flavored with lemon juice. Frederick drank a grape Nehi and I a Co' Cola. Daddy enjoyed a drink of water from the artesian well, whose sulfur flavor pleased him—and me. We took the opportunity to use the restrooms, labeled "White Ladies," "White Men," and "Colored." Once on this drive, when we stopped as usual, our little dog Karo was with us. We let him out of the car for his own bathroom break, and somehow, we left without him, not realizing he had not hopped back into the car. Before too many miles, we missed him and returned to find him.

Occasionally, the Goat Man would be traveling the same road. The Goat Man traveled in a cloth-sided wagon, pulled by goats. He was bearded and wore overalls and a plaid shirt. Accompanied by about twenty goats, some of them wearing clanking bells, he traveled the South, camping in various towns along the way. His caravan was a traffic stopper, and we stared in fascination as Daddy inched the car forward among the bleating goats. I've since learned his name was Ches McCartney. He left a farm in Iowa after the Great Depression and for thirty-eight years wandered along the nation's highways.

During the long drive, in the absence of audiobooks and video games, Mother occupied us by playing counting and word games with us. Counting cows was a favorite; each of us counted the animals on our side of the road. Spotting a white horse was worth extra points. And the real bonus was for seeing a three-legged dog, which actually happened at least once. We also looked for the letters of the alphabet in sequence on the roadside signs. Qs and Zs were hardest to find. Before the trip was over, we often fell asleep as the car purred over the soothing vibrations of road sections, the railroad crossings, and various bumps. The best sleep there is.

A Fertile Land

Although my family by no means lived off the land, we did enjoy its bounty. Native Islanders, on the other hand, had been cut off from the mainland for generations, during which time they survived largely by their own hands. Beside nearly every house, the homeowner cultivated a small garden patch. They planted corn, turnip greens, sweet potatoes, peas, beans, and melons. Along roadsides and paths, wild blackberries and plums grew. Everyone picked and enjoyed those. We children were usually impatient and didn't wait for the fruit, which grew wild along Honey Horn Lane, to ripen. My mouth still draws up at the thought of those *almost*-ripe plums.

Mr. Armstrong, and later Mr. Taylor, planted a garden at Honey Horn. In it they, too, grew corn, butter beans, green beans, squash, okra, watermelons, and cantaloupes. Particularly delicious were the cantaloupes. As Mother cut and prepared cantaloupes for us to eat, she set aside their seeds to dry on paper towels, saving them for the next year's planting. Okra was added to canned tomatoes to make delicious okra and tomatoes, which we ate over rice—a staple food for us. Mr. Taylor also grew zinnias and gladiolas, which were beautiful to pick and arrange indoors. Mother had a tall, light-green vase which just suited the glads.

Islanders also raised chickens, guineas, and turkeys, which they supplemented with wild game. They mainly hunted squirrels and rabbits in the woods, snaring or shooting them. And, of course, the rivers and marshes were filled with fish, crabs, and oysters. Boatmen rowed their bateaus out to oyster banks at low tide and hacked off clusters of oysters. With shovels and pitchforks, they loaded them into their boats. Long before we arrived on the Island, the Hudson and Toomer families had opened oyster houses. Harvesters delivered their haul to the factory, where women opened the shells with knives, washed the oysters, and packed them in cans for shipping—packed in ice.

Boats and nets at Paddy's Camp, on Skull Creek.

A planted field in bloom.

Small fish were caught with cast nets, both to eat and to use as bait for larger fish. These men did not buy nets in stores, but made their own, a skill brought by their ancestors from West Africa. It was not unusual to see a woman or a man sitting under a tree with the center of the net tied to a low branch. Patiently, he wove and knotted row after row to form the round net. Completing a net could take weeks of work. Using a cast net was an art as well. The round net had weights around the outer edge; the fisherman must cast it out over the water so it opened into a circle, while holding one end of the cinch string in his teeth. Daddy knew how to cast a net and taught Frederick and Byron how to do it. Daddy sometimes took Frederick and Byron fishing. For some reason, he never took me, and I felt left out.

Another necessary craft, which is also an art form, was basket weaving. This, too, was a skill brought from Africa. The weaver would cut spartina grass from the marshes, spread the reeds on the ground, and let them dry. Palmetto fronds were also cut into strips and dried. Beginning at the bottom, the artisan coiled small sheaths of the reeds into a circle, binding the successive rows with the palmetto strips. Baskets were made in many shapes for various uses. The most skilled basket maker when we moved to the Island was Caesar Johnson. He made beautiful baskets in many shapes and sizes: round, oval, deep, or shallow. I don't believe he made baskets with handles. One of the most beautiful ones Mother bought from him was a fanner, a large, flat basket used for tossing rice into the air so the chaff blew away.

Wild hogs roamed the woods. As development began, an attempt was made to trap and remove them. Men who worked for Daddy built sturdy pens with trapdoors in the woods. It's not clear to me what happened to the pigs after they were trapped, though some were brought to a pen at Honey Horn, presumably so they could be butchered and eaten. Byron recalls that Mr. Pat sometimes let Frederick and him hold the back legs of the babies, who *squealed*! We had a collection of boars' tusks, some as many as four or five inches long.

In 1953, utilizing the new ferry service, Roy Neil and Bill Taylor of C&D Farms began truck-farming tomatoes on the Island. The first fields planted were the two front fields at Honey Horn, one just in front of our house. As the fields were plowed, billows of dust raised by the tractors blew toward the houses and pretty well covered everything. Migrant black workers, bussed in and housed in the black middle school building on Dead Man's Curve, planted young tomato sets. As the plants matured, they were sprayed with insecticides, whose smell permeated our lives. The fieldworkers, wearing straw hats or bandanas around their heads, hoed the fields to remove weeds. While the tomatoes were still green, these workers picked them, inspected them in an assembly line in a shed, and packed them in sturdy wooden boxes, which were loaded onto trucks and ferried off the Island. We could pick and eat as many ripe tomatoes as we wished, as they had no market value. The back porch table, spread with newspaper, was covered with tomatoes. We enjoyed delicious sliced tomato sandwiches on white bread with Miracle Whip spread. Mother canned some tomatoes to use during the winter. But there was a downside: there were more tomatoes than we and our neighbors could use—and the air was soon filled with the odor of tomatoes rotting in the field. The land had produced too much.

Vanishing Paradise

On a late fall afternoon, Mr. Jackson and Mr. Dixon would drop by. Mr. Jackson walked with a limp but had a warm hug. Mr. Dixon was missing the end of his right index finger, which made for a knobby handshake. They often brought a gift of food: North Carolina apples, venison steaks, wild boar sausage, or maybe honey in the comb. They introduced us to the treat of chewing a waxy honeycomb to extract its sweetness. We would all gather around them to hear their news and plans for the season—times of good stories and shared laughter.

The two men came to the Island to open the North Carolina Hunting Club for the arrival of the other members. The club had been incorporated in 1917 as the Hilton Head Agricultural Society. Its members were mill owners, bankers, physicians, and other local leaders from three communities: Gastonia, North Carolina; Clover, South Carolina; and Chattanooga, Tennessee. Only men were members. Though the hunters often arrived in their business suits, they quickly changed to immerse themselves in the wild surroundings. They sought to escape their ordinary world, and were able to do so away from telephones and other modern conveniences. There was nothing to do but hunt, eat hearty meals of wild game, and swap stories and jokes. When the Marines paved the road to the lighthouse in the late 1930s, one of the younger members said he had a bad feeling every time he passed over the paved road. "It marked the beginning of the end of the island paradise."[1]

---

[1] Richard Rankin, *A New South Hunt Club*, 91.

The club owned around two thousand acres of land in the middle of the Island, where Palmetto Dunes Resort is now. As did the rest of us, the club kept vehicles on the Island and had someone meet them when they arrived by boat. The association maintained Camp Dilling, a small compound near Broad Creek. A rustic clubhouse held a living room, dining room, kitchen, and bunk room. Other structures and a trailer accommodated more of the hunters. Dog kennels and various outbuildings completed the layout. A Gullah caretaker and master of the dogs kept an eye on things when none of the hunters were on the Island. During the winter, each group of hunters came for a one-week hunt. Early in the morning, the hunting guide stationed the men on individual deer stands. The hunters generally had good luck, as deer were abundant. Occasionally, they bagged turkeys or a wild hog. After a late lunch, they fished, explored the woods and the beach, perhaps captured an alligator, or just relaxed.

Once or twice during a North Carolina hunting week, Mr. Jackson invited my family to the club for supper. The rules of the club allowed guests of members, at a cost of $1.50 per guest. As we entered the room it was filled with male voices and the smells of smoke from a crackling fire, cigarette and pipe tobacco, and whiskey. We children were not used to being around so many big men at once, and we tried to hide behind Mother. The men in their flannel shirts, canvas pants, snake-proof boots, and with booming voices were overpowering and looked rough. They smiled and spoke kindly to us, quickly putting us at ease, and we had a good time. Everyone sat together at a large table for a dinner of wild game: venison, wild boar, duck, or Brunswick stew. More exotic meats were sometimes served, like alligator tail and rattlesnake fillets. "It tastes like chicken," Mr. Jackson said, and it did. Though a cook from Gastonia came down with the men, Mr. Jackson loved to cook and often took part in preparing the meals. After dinner, we all sang camp songs and hymns as Mr. Jackson played his accordion. After we left, the men may have gone out for a coon hunt. Did any of us realize how quickly this wilderness would be gone?

Fire!

On a crisp winter night, we sit by a dancing flame in the fireplace. It warms us, calms us, makes us drowsy. When Daddy tosses another log onto the fire, sparks shoot up onto the sooty bricks. To me they look like tiny men with lanterns climbing and descending hills in the peaceful dark. Mother finally announces, "Time for bed!" She warms our flannel blankets before the fire, and Frederick and I go to bed, with our feet snugly wrapped.

In the midst of a normal morning in 1950, I wrinkle my nose. "Ooooooh! What's that awful smell?" In the kitchen, I see Louise's strong black arm grasping the webbed feet of a scrawny, featherless duck. Quickly she lowers it right into the flames of the big, black wood stove, to singe off those pesky pinfeathers that remain after plucking the feathers.

In the night there's a knock on the door. "There's a fire in the woods!" And Daddy's off into the blackness. The logging crews gather with rubber fire flaps and shovels to face a roaring, rolling wall of heat. Sweaty faces glow red and hair is singed from hands and arms, but the fighters can't give up. Rising wind adds to the fire's own force. Seemingly a living thing, it rushes toward them. How can flaps and shovels stop or even slow this primal force?

Woods fires were one of the few crimes committed on the Island. Daddy was always on the lookout, as a fire could quickly destroy acres of timber. Firebreaks were regularly plowed through the woods to prevent, or at least slow, their spread. Some fires were naturally or accidentally started, possibly by lightning or by rabbit or squirrel hunters in the woods, warming their hands on a chilly night. There were also moonshiners, who set up their stills in the woods. Their fires could get out of control. But at other times, fires were deliberately set. Some of the old-timers resented "outsiders" coming to the Island and changing the way things had been for a century.

There were night hunters in the woods as well. Locating deer at night while riding in a vehicle and using a spotlight to reflect their eyes was illegal. I hope it still is. The deer were blinded and immobilized by the light shining in their eyes, making them easy targets. Daddy would join Mr. Pat and Mr. Taylor and the three of them would set out to round up those responsible. With their pistols tucked in their waistbands, they would drive into the woods looking for other vehicles moving about. To improve their stealthy approach, they turned their headlights off and removed the bulbs from the overhead lights so they would not come on if the door was opened. The aim was to surprise these men in the act and arrest them. After they appeared in the magistrate's court, they were turned over to the sheriff's department on the mainland. In 1953, Mr. Pat was appointed magistrate and was consistently reelected from then on. Mr. Taylor was a constable. So they were the "law" on the Island.

We children could help in spotting another kind of lawbreaker: shrimpers running their boats too close to the shore, with their nets lowered. They were probably used to Hilton Head Island being sparsely inhabited so no one would notice their disregard for the regulation prohibiting trawling close to shore. It was exciting to us to try to spot and identify the boats. To report them, one had to be able to read the name on the boat. The crew quickly covered the name with a burlap sack when they noticed someone on shore with binoculars. Since we spied on them from a distance, we were in no danger.

The search for lawbreakers gave a frontier feel to our life.

Going to Town

Savannah was our town.[2] To this day, "going to town" brings to mind the trip to Savannah. Mother had spent part of her childhood there and had continued to make it her city base—whether from Townsend, Clyo, Hinesville, or finally Hilton Head Island. We went to Savannah for everything: food, laundry, clothing, doctors, dentist, Daddy's haircuts and Mother's permanents, and library books. None of these was available on the Island. We three children were all born at the Telfair Memorial Hospital in Savannah.

"Rise and shine! We're going to town today." Mother woke us for the day's adventure. While we ate breakfast at the dining room table, she counted the laundry, listing each item in a notebook. She stuffed all the sheets, pillowcases, towels, and Daddy's shirts into a heavy cotton bag, soft from many washings, and tucked a copy of the list into the top. In the kitchen, she made sandwiches in case we were hungry on the two-hour journey—or in case the ferry was delayed. Our sandwiches were butter (oleo) and sugar on *white bread*, each sandwich wrapped in wax paper. For herself, Mother poured hot coffee into a thermos. "Let me find the lists from Mrs. Taylor and Margaret and we're ready to go. OK, into the car now!"

After the trip to the mainland by boat, or later ferry, Mother drove through Bluffton and Pritchardville and onto Highway 17, the Coastal Highway. As we crossed the marsh through the Savannah River Reserve, Mother pointed out coots (which looked

---

[2] Apologies to Isak Dinesen, *Out of Africa*, 10.

like small black ducks) on the water. There might be red-tailed hawks or sparrow hawks (now American kestrels) on the power poles, scanning for prey; and often we saw cottontail rabbits along the edges of the highway.

As we entered Port Wentworth, the smell of Union Camp Paper Mill filled the car. Phew! "The people who live here say it smells like money," Mother assured us. Though I didn't care for the smell, it's one I always recognize. We stopped there at the White Way Laundry to drop our bundle and pick up the clean sheets and towels, along with Daddy's shirts, washed, ironed, and folded around rectangular shirt cardboards. All were packaged in brown paper and tied with string. At home in the evening, Mother opened the packages, carefully untying the knots and winding the string into a ball to use later.

The drive to Savannah from Buckingham Landing took about an hour. In 1953, with the opening of the Talmadge Memorial Bridge over the Savannah River, US Highway 17A opened. Fairly soon, Daddy learned another "shortcut," which ran from US Highway 17 through the community of Levy, and joined US 17A just before it crossed the marshes to the new bridge. This new route reduced the driving time by fifteen minutes or more.

A Day in Savannah

The viaduct over the railroad tracks dumped us onto Bay Street in downtown Savannah. Mother turned onto Broughton Street, where the stores were: Levy's and Adler's department stores; Fine's for ladies clothing; Kress's, Woolworth's, and McCrory's five- and ten-cent stores. Mother might look for fabric and patterns. We sometimes had a little money—a dollar as a birthday or Christmas gift, a few nickels earned by shelling butter beans and peas. We chose small things, a coin purse, a toy soldier, or a comic book.

At noon, Mother took us to Morrison's Cafeteria, which was a highlight of the day. There we were allowed to select our own food as we pushed our trays along the rails in front of the array of foods: salads, desserts (yes, the sweets came early in the display), meats and vegetables, breads, and drinks. We could reach across and pick up the dish of food we wanted—except for the meat, which a server sliced and placed on a plate. The boys and I always selected carrot-and-raisin salad and the corn sticks with little butter pats on tiny white, porcelain plates. Mother's favorite was the custard pie. After we had filled our trays and the cashier had totaled up the bill, a waiter carried the trays to a table covered with a white tablecloth. The silver-plated flatware was wrapped in white cloth napkins. Under each corner of the table was a small hook on which a lady could hang her pocketbook. For us, this was elegant dining.

Mother and Avary on Broughton Street, Savannah, Georgia, ca. 1950.

Occasionally, we went by to visit Aunt Janie, Grandfather's sister, at the Graham Apartments, a block off Broughton Street. We called our uncles and aunts by their first names and our great-uncles and aunts *Aunt* Janie, etc. I suppose we copied what Mother and Daddy called them. Aunt Janie had never married; instead, she stayed home to care for their ailing mother until her death. Then she showered her love on her nieces, nephew, and great-nieces and nephews. Aunt Janie had a tiny efficiency apartment, which was truly efficient. It was one room with a small bathroom. The kitchen consisted of a two-burner cooktop, refrigerator, and one cabinet, located in a corner of the room. Next to the bed was a pine cabinet, with a door which folded down to form a table. Shelves inside the door held Aunt Janie's few dishes, which were washed in the bathroom sink after a meal. Sometimes she kept us while Mother went to the beauty parlor or on some other errand. Even better was a visit to Aunt Janie's office, where she would let me type on her typewriter. Aunt Janie was a dear, unselfish lady. Though she had little, she generously shared with us and others. When I was born in 1945, she gave me (Mother) ten dollars, a rather princely sum then, which must have strained her budget. I cherish several cards and a few letters she wrote me, beginning when I was a newborn. In a letter she wrote (typed) me for my eighth birthday:

> *Eight years ago when you came to live with Mother and Daddy, we were all so happy. You were just a "mite" of humanity then, but how we loved you! What a big girl this little mite has become. We have never ceased to be thankful that you came, and have watched and loved you as you grew bigger and bigger. [I] remember how you looked on your first celebration, as you reached your little hands out to touch your cake. Everyone beamed with pride.*

Another favorite part of our trip was a visit to the public library. Mother left us browsing through the children's department, where we sat on the floor in front of the shelves and leafed through book after book. Mother searched the adult stacks for books she hadn't read. She was quickly working her way through the supply! Then she helped us make final selections. We each had our own library card, so we checked out our own books, leaving with our arms loaded.

The last stop was the grocery store, most memorably the A&P on Abercorn Street. Mother preferred their Eight O'Clock Coffee—still one I favor. In the checkout lane, the cashier ground the coffee beans and repackaged them in the same bright-red bag. A grocery boy packed at least a week's worth of groceries into sturdy cardboard boxes, which were easier to handle than paper bags. Mother had a large cooler for "meat," which was basically synonymous with "beef." Other meats included canned corned beef hash, Spam, Vienna sausage, and deviled ham. Mother often cooked corned beef hash with poached eggs. She spread the hash in a pan, made depressions, and cracked an egg into each, before putting the pan into the oven. I still like this dish. She believed pork wasn't good for us. Perhaps it was more dangerous because of the distance we had to travel home. Chickens were raised at Honey Horn.

Magical Worlds

We went to Savannah most years for two special events: the Coastal Empire Fair and the Ringling Bros. Barnum & Bailey Circus. One year, Mr. and Mrs. McGinty took the school to the fair as a field trip—all five of us!

The main attractions at the fair were cotton candy and the midway rides. We walked through the exhibition barns displaying livestock and compared the prizewinning pigs to those Orion had raised at Hacks Pasture in Hinesville. The horses held some interest for us, since we had and rode horses. We wanted to pet each one. The warm smells, stamping, and snuffling in the livestock barns were familiar and reassuring. But the exhibits of jellies, jams, preserves, pies, and cakes were of no interest at all.

We were eager to get to the merry-go-round and bumper cars.

The best time for the rides was after dark when the lights created a fairy-tale world. As we walked along the midway, sounds came from every side: hawkers shouted to lure us into their sideshows, loud music came from every exhibit, and people on the rides screamed. We always thought we'd ride the Ferris wheel, but when it came to getting into the swaying gondola, we usually backed out. There were booths to test one's marksmanship—both with a loud rifle (surely these were not real bullets!) and by throwing rings over bottles. The prizes were unnaturally colored stuffed animals. In an open sawdust-floored tent, we tried to win a dish by tossing a dime into it. Sometimes Daddy won a platter or pretty bowl Mother could actually use.

Only after the unsettling rides did Mother allow us to have food—cotton candy, weenies, candied apples—followed by the fear of being carsick on the way home.

The circus was a different experience, filled with magic. We heard about but never saw the parade through downtown Savannah, when the animals were unloaded from the circus train and walked or were pulled in cages to the tent. The midway shows amazed us: men swallowing swords or eating fire—and the midgets! They were tiny, perfectly formed people. The adults were about the size of us children, wearing child-sized adult clothes. The ladies even had tiny high-heeled shoes! We were innocents, unaware that the circus managers were taking unfair advantage of these little people because of their diminutive size. Blessedly, we never saw any real "freaks" in the sideshows.

Finally the moment came to enter the Big Top and find our seats. The floor was covered with sawdust and the air filled with dust and the chatter and laughter of the excited crowd. Accompanied by shrilling calliope music, the animals and performers paraded into the tent, around and into the three performing rings: beautifully dressed ladies with long plumes on their heads rode Asian elephants; roustabouts pulled cages of tigers or lions followed by their powerful, whip-cracking trainers; white horses pranced in wearing their own flowing plumes on their heads;

clowns tripped over their own feet; and exotic trapeze artists and gymnasts, in tight-fitting but glittering costumes, stepped gracefully along.

The Ringmaster, wearing a striped cutaway coat and black top hat, strutted into the center ring, stepped onto a colorful platform, and blew three loud blasts on his whistle. The crowd hushed and the show began! The action circulated from ring to ring: the acrobatic elephants sitting and balancing on their feet to turn on large barrels; the bareback riders standing on galloping horses; the trapeze artists leaping from swing to swing; and tightrope walkers high in the air, above nets that would catch them if they lost their balance. A knife thrower tossed his wicked-looking blades, barely missing his gaudily dressed assistant with her arms spread before a target. Another beauty was sawn in two before our eyes. Dogs performed tricks, leaping through rings and over barriers.

Clowns performed their silly antics to distract us while the scenes changed. One year, we saw the sad Emmett Kelly, whom Mother told us was a famous clown. I've recently done some research and learned Mr. Kelly began his career as a trapeze artist in 1923, but became a clown full time in 1931. By the time we saw him, he had convinced management to allow him to leave his role as a white-face clown, performing slapstick humor. He developed the hobo clown, Weary Willie, a tragic figure with which his Depression-era audiences identified. One of his skits the year we saw him involved his sweeping the rings between acts. He tried to sweep away a pool of light from a spotlight, but, of course, failed, to the delight of the audience. We must have seen him in 1955, as my research shows he took the 1956 season off to perform as the Brooklyn Dodgers' mascot.

Perhaps the highlight, though, was the lion tamer. Wearing a khaki safari suit and pith helmet, he strode into the center ring cracking his whip. One by one, he unlocked the cages and the fierce cats leapt out. Some jumped through rings—occasionally, flaming rings. Finally, all the lions would be loping in a circle and sitting on barrels at his command. I blush to think I could enjoy such a spectacle which exploited these magnificent beasts.

As we left the fairgrounds, we purchased a final cotton candy and a circus souvenir: a flimsy fuchsia walking stick with colored feathers on the top; a striped twirling baton with glitter-encrusted knobs; a round, red clown's nose; or plastic animals. On the way home, I pondered, "I think I'll be a circus performer when I grow up—or maybe an animal trainer."

Frederick added, "That would be fun. Traveling with the show and living in a little trailer."

"And we would be in new places every day!" I said.

"With all those cute animals," added Byron.

"It wouldn't be as much fun as you think," Mother said. "Moving all the time isn't easy. You would never have a home."

In May 2017, Ringling Bros. Barnum & Bailey Circus folded its tents for the final time.

Easter Joys

B yron came to us at Easter—or that's the first time Frederick and I saw him. He was born on Monday, April 7, 1952; the following Sunday was Easter. Nana and Grandfather had kept us at their house at the Ridge while Mother spent a couple of weeks at the Whitney Hotel in Savannah, before going to the Telfair Memorial Hospital. She could not risk waiting on the Island until the last minute before taking a boat to the mainland, followed by the long ride to Savannah. Nana dressed us in our Easter outfits. I was almost seven and wore a navy-blue suit—pleated skirt and bolero jacket, with a white blouse. I probably had a little straw hat, more like a wide headband with a little bunch of small nylon flowers and ribbon trim. Frederick, four and a half, wore navy pants, a white shirt, and a clip-on tie.

Because it was Easter, children were allowed into the maternity ward in the afternoon. After we saw Mother in her room, Daddy took us down the hall, where through a large plate-glass window, we saw the cribs in the nursery. As a nurse lifted Byron and held him near the window, Daddy pointed and said, "There's your new brother." On his chubby arm, he wore a bracelet of tiny blue-and-white beads bearing the letters H A C K.

"He's so little," whispered Frederick.

"And so *cute*!" I added. Daddy beamed.

Byron recalls: "Once I saw a diary Daddy kept for a very brief time in which he recorded that Mose Hudson came to the house one morning (7:30 a.m., I think) to tell him of my arrival. He took Daddy over to Buckingham Landing so he could drive to Savannah. I don't remember seeing the diary again." The loss of Daddy's diaries is a mystery and leaves a gap in Island history.

Following the family tradition of difficult names displaying our genealogy, Mother and Daddy named their new son Orion Byron for his grandfather, George Byron Hack, and his uncle, Orion Davis Hack. "We won't call him 'Orion,'" Mother said, "because Orion may have a son of his own." Her prediction was correct: fifteen years later, Orion Davis Hack, Jr., was born to a fifty-year-old father and his beautiful young wife, Alicia.

Besides the blue suit, I remember one other store-bought Easter dress—pink organdy with small white flowers printed on it. Nana made most of my Easter dresses, as well as most of my other clothes. One of my favorite dresses Nana made was of white polished cotton with red polka dots. It was long-waisted with short sleeves and a square neck. The skirt was full enough that I wore a crinoline under it. Crinolines were petticoats of layered tiers of scratchy net. When starched, they really poofed out a dress! Often Nana made more than one dress from a pattern, as she did with this Easter pattern. The other was of a plaid fabric, suitable to wear to school.

Each Easter, Mother helped me choose new white shoes, lace-trimmed socks (until I was finally old enough to wear stockings), pocketbook, hat, and short, white, cotton gloves. Unfortunately, these beautiful outfits required a sweater or jacket. Whereas every Christmas seemed too warm, Easter was too cold. I remember one white sweater, decorated with tiny "pearls." Another year, Dianne and I both had short white nylon "fur" jackets with three-quarter sleeves.

Every year, when we were all dressed up, Frederick, Byron, Dianne, and I stood in front of a car to have our picture taken with our parents' Kodak Brownie cameras. Some pictures show Mother's car, others the Taylors' car—but always a Chevrolet. Did we pose with the cars because we were ready for church? At least it serves as a time marker. Exhorted to "Face into the sun," we are always squinting in photographs.

Byron's second birthday, 1954.

Avary in her Easter outfit, 1954.

The Easter Bunny was a pretty big deal, though no match for Santa Claus. At bedtime, we left our baskets, empty except for some green wax paper grass, on the dining room table. In the morning, they were filled with jelly beans, coconut cream eggs, and chocolate eggs. One special chocolate egg had a little window; putting my eye close to the hole, I could see a bunny inside. When we were very young, maybe still in Hinesville, the Easter Bunny left two molded cardboard rabbits with baskets of candy on their backs—mine a little larger than Frederick's, as it should be. Their ears are slightly chewed. Did we think they were candy? Another time, we received large plastic eggs filled with candy. My egg is pink with little blue flowers painted on top; Frederick's is yellow with a large red flower. I can describe these so clearly because I still have them—in my original Easter basket.

One year in Hinesville, Daddy took Frederick and me to the feed store and let us select pink, green, and blue biddies, little balls of fluff. They quickly outgrew their cardboard box and became chickens. I have a feeling they ended up as chicken 'n dumplin's after mysterious disappearances. Mother really could not abide birds around her, so allowing these Easter chicks in the house was a real gift to us. To her relief, such frivolous choices were not available on the Island.

A day or two before Easter, Dianne came over and we dyed eggs. Mother dropped the dye tablets into custard cups and dissolved them in vinegar and boiling water. We tried to lower the hard-boiled eggs into the cups, using the flimsy wire hoops provided. Most dropped off and cracked, so the dye ended up staining the whites. Each package of Easter-egg dye included thin tissue sheets with images printed on them: lilies, rabbits, butterflies, and crosses. We followed the directions to "press the tissue onto the egg with a warm damp cloth until the image is transferred." The results were hardly recognizable. Perfect or not, after church or Sunday School on Easter Sunday, the eggs were hidden in the yard: nestled in a clump of grass, under a palmetto frond or a fallen sycamore leaf, or beside the brick edging of the oyster shell front walk. Some were so easy to find that Frederick, Dianne, and I knew they were meant for Byron, still a toddler, and we left them for him. After finding all the eggs, we begged Daddy to hide them again. And he did.

Sunrise services didn't begin on the Island until the Baptist church was organized, shortly after the bridge to the Island opened. The Baptists had a choir and could sing, somberly:

> *Low in the grave he lay, Jesus my Savior;*
> *Waiting the coming day, Jesus my Lord!*

And then, with a stirring beat:

> *Up from the grave He arose,*
> *With a mighty triumph o'er His foes.*

The services were held on the sand dunes at the beach, among the sea oats. The sun rising over the ocean was beautiful, but the sand gnats often dominated the morning.

In earlier years, Mother taught us the story of Jesus' resurrection, using a flannel-graph board, on which we recreated the story as she read, adding and rearranging figures as the events unfolded. First, the three women approached the tomb with the rock sealing its opening. Then the angel appeared and removed the rock. Finally, the risen Jesus appeared, and the women ran with the Good News to the disciples—and we learned it, too.

Trick or Treat!

I remember no Hallowe'ens before we moved from Hinesville. But from our first year on the Island, Hallowe'en was special. We were taught to spell it that way, with an apostrophe, since it is a contraction of All Hallows' Even.

In these years, there were few neighbors for us to visit, but Mother created costumes for us, which changed little from year to year. Mother dressed me as a gypsy in scarves with large gold loop (clip) earrings, and she painted my lips with her bright red lipstick. One year she made a skirt and shawl for me of white cotton material with a pattern of red cats with large yellow eyes. As I grew, Mother let out the hem in the skirt, and eventually added a plain yellow band at the top to make it even longer. The long, narrow shawl was fringed on the ends, a favorite finish she used to avoid hemming. I helped her make napkins like this: she cut squares of fabric, stitched them about half an inch from the edge (sometimes in a contrasting color), and I pulled threads out of the edges, making the fringe. This was apparently a style of the times.

Frederick was a clown or a pirate. As a clown, he had a store-bought costume, with a round, red nose and a painted face. His pirate costume was cut-off shorts, an eye patch, his tricorn hat from the Midway bicentennial celebration where we had all dressed in colonial costumes, and a plastic sword. As he grew older, he added one earring and tied a bandana around his head. Byron later wore the clown suit.

After dark, we set out, Frederick and I carrying orange cardboard jack-o'-lanterns, with wax candles burning in them. We walked across the road to the Armstrongs' house. The oyster shells covering the front walk crunched under our feet as we passed between tall magnolia trees, with their limbs reaching all the way to the ground. The large leaves rustled. "What's that?" Then we passed round cedars which cast spooky shadows. Mother and Daddy followed with a flashlight, which enlarged our shadows and made them move across our path.

When we reached the door and knocked, the response to our "Trick or treat!" was candy corn (which I still love!), an apple, or silver tips (a.k.a. Hershey's Kisses). One year, as we turned back down the walkway, my shawl dipped into my jack-o'-lantern and burst into flames! Daddy quickly pulled it from my shoulders and put out the fire. No great damage was done. Mother trimmed the shawl and I refringed it. But that was the last year we used real candles!

Daddy drove us to Mrs. Merritt's house on Honey Horn Lane. She rewarded us with homemade treats: cookies or fudge. Finally, Daddy took us to Miss Milley's at the far end of the field. Her yard was filled with sprawling azalea bushes and shaded by large, moss-draped oaks, so that lacy shadows moved across it. *And* she had two barking dogs—a muscular boxer and a springy cocker spaniel. But she called to them and calmed them so we could open her gate and walk to the front door. She, too, rewarded us with a treat.

When Mrs. McGinty came to the Island in 1954 to be our teacher, Hallowe'en reached new heights. She and her husband, Pete, created sophisticated decorations and organized a school carnival on Hallowe'en Day. In preparation, we each made a papier-mâché mask, using wet newspaper and lots of paste, which we painted when it was thoroughly dry. We decorated the classroom with creations we traced from patterns and cut from construction paper: black cats, orange pumpkins, witches on brooms, and black-and-orange paper chains. On the big day, parents of all five students and Byron, who was too young for school, were invited to the party—in costume.

Mrs. McGinty arranged games, which we played for prizes.

With our hands clasped behind our backs we bobbed for apples in a large galvanized washtub of water—courageous, if you had a loose tooth. I can't remember who had this loose tooth, but it sounds painful. Using a tiny fishing pole and hook, we fished for small plastic fish floating in another washtub. We tied a scarf over each other's eyes and played blind man's bluff, and took turns pinning the tail on the donkey. Wet and happy, everyone ate cupcakes, topped with black and orange confectioner's sugar icing.

On Hallowe'en night, we approached the McGintys' house. It was in total darkness—or was that a flickering light inside? Their car was parked in the driveway, so they had to be home. As we knocked, creaking and moaning filled the night, the door silently opened, and through the pale light of a cobweb-veiled room, a ghost swooped from the ceiling to meet us face to face. An ugly witch with a mole on her nose and a peaked black hat came forward and in reply to our weak "Trick or treat" demanded the *trick*! We were startled and taken by surprise. After our initial hesitation, Mrs. McGinty invited us in for some of her iced cookies and hot cider.

Hosts of Angels

Before moving to the Island, we had spent our Christmases with Nana and Grandfather. For a few years, we still made this journey from Hilton Head Island. What a hassle it must have been for Mother and Daddy to pack all Santa's surprises without our knowing about it, though I suppose we paid little attention to what went into suitcases and boxes. Perhaps Nana had bought things, or maybe Mother had ordered from catalogues and had things shipped to the Ridge. But Santa never failed to find us wherever we were—even though we worried because Nana and Grandfather's fireplaces were boarded over. Though I don't remember this from the time, on my very first Christmas one of my gifts was a pink plush elephant, whom I named Ellie. I credit Ellie as the basis of my ongoing passion for elephants—and by extension, Africa. Another year, a friend of Nana's gave me a blond, plush horse, whom I named Bobbie, after a horse Grandfather had named Bobbin. Bobbie stayed at the house on the Ridge for many years. As the years passed, and they were excessively loved, Mother had to fashion new coverings for both: Ellie in pink corduroy and Bobbie in pink-and-white striped cotton. I took Ellie to Agnes Scott College when I went, and still keep him on the bed.

After dinner on Christmas Day, we visited Grandmother in Hinesville, which was only a short drive from the Ridge. She insisted we eat another full Christmas dinner with her, Orion, and Jane. Grandmother was certainly loving and always selected gifts which were uniquely appropriate and pleasing: a music box, panties with lace trim, or baby-doll pajamas for me; pretty stationery for Mother.

A Christmas Tree

"When will it get cold?"
"Will we have snow?"
"It's supposed to snow at Christmas!"

In spite of our wishes, Christmas in the South was almost always warm, but magical.

One afternoon, Daddy would come home and say, "Let's go get a tree!" We all climbed into the car to search the woods for a Christmas tree. No fir or hemlock—and few cedars—grew on the Island, so we always selected a longleaf pine. Trees with the best shape usually grew in old firebreaks or overgrown fields, where the branches could spread freely. Daddy drove along woods roads until we found a stand of pines which looked about the right size. Then we walked among the trees, studying them from all sides.

"This one looks good!"
"No, the top is broken."
"I like that one over there!"
"No, no! There're no limbs on this side."

When everyone finally agreed we had found the perfect one, Daddy chopped it down with his axe. As we all "helped" drag it to the car, we got sticky, fresh, Christmas-smelling pine sap all over our hands and often our jeans and shirts. When the tree was loaded into the trunk of Daddy's Chevy sedan, we went happily home, humming Christmas carols.

After Daddy secured the tree in its stand and situated it in the corner of the living room, it never failed that, in spite of our careful selection in the woods, there were several gaps in the branches. But eventually, Daddy turned it to its best advantage, anchored it to the wall with wires, and we started decorating it. First, Daddy put the tinsel star at the very top, secured one bulb from the first string of lights in its center, and began to string the large, colored lights and bubbling candles among the branches. Each brilliantly colored candlelight was composed of a translucent glass taper which rose from a plastic base, both of which contained oil. When the light was clipped to a branch so it was *perfectly* vertical, bubbles rose through the oil in the taper.

Though Daddy insisted on handling the lights himself, we all hung ornaments. Believe me, hanging things on a longleaf pine is tricky—either the branch is too limp to hold anything, or the ornament is lost among the fifteen-inch needles. Finally, the tree was covered with painted glass birds with bristling tails, shiny glass balls in brilliant colors, bells, foil cones, a painted glass Santa—and a few red-and-green construction-paper chains we'd made at school. Last, we added the silver, cellophane icicles. Mother and Daddy usually put these on after we were sent to bed, because we tried to throw them onto the tree by handfuls, not having the patience to hang each one separately. Daddy, on the other hand, used a yardstick to patiently situate the individual icicles onto the top branches.

Mother decorated the living room mantel with shiny, green magnolia leaves. In its center, Daddy secured branches of silvered driftwood into a square concrete block to form a tree. Across its branches Mother draped multicolored garlands of small glass beads. Beneath the tree stood a dainty plastic angel choir holding harps, violins, and trumpets; a whimsical, wooden group of cherubs with accordions and banjos; and a trio of larger straw angels, which Orion had brought from one of his trips to Mexico. Once friends knew Mother liked angels, they began to give them to her, and without intending to she had a growing collection. As the angels multiplied, they migrated into and took over the branches of the tree, which became the "Angel Tree."

Unpacking (and repacking!) all the angels became a pleasant tradition. Mother remembered who had given her each one, and marked most of the boxes to help us all remember.

"Oh, Nancy brought me that one from Italy! . . . I bought this one in Oberammergau! That was such fun. Bettie went with me on that trip. . . . Tim and Betsy painted these sand dollars! . . . Betty made this one in the brocade gown." Daddy gave her two golden foil angels enclosed in clear glass teardrop globes. Friends brought crafted artifacts from their European travels or folk-art creations from closer to home. Dianne gave her a cherub made of a large cotton boll; its stem serves as a halo and it wears burlap wings. Various Island friends painted angels on sea shells. Some made of cardboard or foil became so misshapen over the years, they had only sentimental value. No matter the physical attributes of the angel, Mother declared with great authority that all angels are male.

As Mother grew older, she needed more help to repackage the angels—but had lots of advice for helpers about exactly which box each belonged in! "No, that is where the cotton boll goes. . . . Put the clam-shell angel in the red box." The Angel Tree stood decorated longer and longer each year. In fact, when Mother died in March 1998, it still reigned on the dogtrot. Below was the manger scene with its international menagerie of exotic beasts—in addition to camels and sheep, there were an elephant, a zebra, and a hippopotamus, a replica of "William," the blue Egyptian hippo from the Metropolitan Museum of Art. The angels kept guard over all.

The Littlest Angel

In the two years Aileen McGinty was our teacher, the entire school performed in a Christmas play: an elaborate production of *The Littlest Angel*, which Mrs. McGinty adapted from Charles Tazewell's classic. In preparation, we five students created golden halos and gilded harps from shirt cardboards. Cut and pasted, the halos were sprayed gold. Mr. McGinty hung white sheets from wires across the front of the classroom, which served as stage curtains and formed a background of clouds. Gold and silver stars dotted the sheets; occasionally a star drifted down to the streets of heaven. A golden harp hung among the stars, marking the spot where the angels, draped in sheets and sporting golden cardboard wings on their backs, gathered for nightly prayers.

The Littlest Angel *production cast, left to right: Avary, Bernadette, Gracie (in front), Frederick, Dianne, 1954.*

On the big night, the lights were dimmed. The audience sat silently in awe. A hush fell. Then Mrs. McGinty read lines from Tazewell's book: "Once upon a time—oh, many, many years ago as time is calculated by men . . . there was, in Paradise, a most miserable, thoroughly unhappy, utterly dejected cherub who was known throughout Heaven as The Littlest Angel." With his short robe askew and his halo "slipping down over his right eye—or over his left eye," our hero entered stage left, walking carefully to be sure no splinters pierced his socked feet. An evening of perfect magic unfolded.

The Littlest Angel was played by the first-grader each year.

The older students played the Gate-Keeper, Mary, and Joseph—wearing the traditional bathrobes and towel turbans—and doubled as angels. The only "spoken" parts (other than the Voice of God!) were the songs of the Celestial Choir, sung to the accompaniment of the pump organ. During rehearsals, Mrs. McGinty instructed the Choir to look above the audience's heads into the corner of the room above the cloakroom door as we sang "It Came Upon the Midnight Clear." I still gaze up and to the left when I sing this carol.

Finally, Mary, Joseph, and the angels knelt in adoration before the manger, as the audience of eighteen watched spellbound—just as they had the year before. Into the stillness boomed the voice of God: "Of all the gifts of all the angels, I find that this small box pleases Me most." The shabby brown box lying before the manger of the Christ Child transformed into a Heavenly light and rose slowly to become the Star of Bethlehem.

When school was out for the holidays, Mother, Dianne, and I "polished the silver." While we used the sterling silver flatware daily, the silver tea service, bowls, and trays appeared only at Christmas and for other special occasions. Mother's silver was either family pieces received as wedding gifts or inexpensive Mexican silver. She had a passion for silver and visited silver shops just to browse. When she could afford it, she bought miscellaneous items. While I was in college, she located a complete set of Stieff Rose flatware in an antique shop, and insisted I buy it! Gerry and I use it daily.

We pulled each item from its brown, Pacific cloth covering and industriously rubbed it with Hagerty's pink polish. While we worked, we talked about other Christmases, what we expected Santa Claus to bring, and the Christmas Eve party and visits with relatives.

Nana made syrup candy. She poured cane syrup into a pot and

heated it with butter and then pulled the mixture by hand until it reached a fairly firm consistency. We liked to help with the prolonged pulling. Then each piece was twisted into a small square of wax paper. Mrs. Taylor made divinity. This was a fluffy, creamy confection made from stiffly beaten egg whites and sugar, with some pecan pieces mixed in. Even when we were very young, we helped Mother make peanut butter cookies, smashing a crisscross design into the top of each with a fork. Mrs. Merritt and Mrs. McGinty both made beautifully decorated and delicious sugar cookies, in the shapes of candy canes, snowmen, angels, and stars, and decorated them either with colored icing or sugar and silver sprinkles. Every year, Mrs. McGinty baked each family one of her light fruitcakes, filled with golden and black raisins, pecans, and currants. She wrapped the cakes in whisky-soaked cloths and sealed them in aluminum foil. The recipe remains her family secret.

Mother gathered Frederick, Byron, and me around the dining room table to wrap presents for our grandparents, aunts, and uncles—and for Daddy. These gifts were uninteresting to us: handkerchiefs, socks, bath powder, stationery, and postage stamps. I now realize money was scarce and the gifts we exchanged were needed and useful. My favorite wrapping motif was white tissue paper over either red or green tissue, tied with curled crinkle ribbon of the same color. No gift bags in those days! Mother delayed her wrapping till after the Christmas Eve party and stayed up most of the night. This was finally her quiet time.

What a treat it was when the Sears Roebuck and Montgomery Ward Christmas catalogs arrived in the mail! We created our Christmas wish lists from their toy pages, since without television, we were not tempted by ads. Armed with these lists, we were ready when the night came for a trip to Savannah. Mother and Daddy packed us all into the car—our uncle Orion usually went with us—and we took the boat across to Buckingham Landing. After an hour's drive, we finally reached Savannah. Daddy drove down Broughton Street, where we stared through the car windows at lighted garlands hung over the street. Every store window was bright and filled with "snowy" scenes and tempting Christmas treasures. After Daddy found a vacant parking space, we skipped along Broughton Street to Adler's department store, jostled by other shoppers as eager as we. One of Santa's helpers, dressed just like Santa Claus, sat in a comfortable chair in the toy department. He smiled and held out his arms to take each child onto his knee, where we *whispered* our Christmas wishes into his ear—having added a few items spotted as we walked through the dazzling toy department displays.

Before heading home, Daddy drove us around town "to see the lights." We hoped people had left their curtains open so we could see their trees—rating each one by oohs and ahhs. The last treat was to ride around Forsyth Park. Each year, the city erected a huge tree. It must have been thirty feet tall. City employees used fire ladder-trucks to string large, colored lights and place the star at the top. The result was breathtaking and visible from all sides of Savannah's largest park.

The next day, Mother would insist we each write a letter to Santa Claus as well. She was quite a letter writer and took every opportunity to encourage this habit. That evening after the letters were done, we floated them up the chimney over the fire. They magically found their way to the North Pole.

Santa Claus Is Real!

Everyone looked forward to Mother's Christmas Eve party. In my naive child's mind, I thought everyone on the Island came, but there were other residents who were not part of this group, which included only the Honey Horn residents and a few Island friends and others who might be visiting—maybe twenty of us.

Dianne, Gracie, and I wore velveteen dresses and black patent leather shoes. The men wore their red Christmas ties and vests. Mother always wore a string of chartreuse Christmas beads, wrapped around her neck against a creamy blouse, and a green brocade skirt. Recently, one of Aileen McGinty's daughters shared a poem written by her mother, which described the black mules Mother wore:

Unrequited Longing

Each Christmas Eve
We went to a gathering of families
In a wonderfully jumbled house.
It was a country party
Where we played games, sang carols,
Helped the hostess deck the tree.

One year she wore an early gift:
A pair of slippers
Black velvet, with tiny golden bells
Swinging from the hollow of their heels.
At the Christmas party from then on
Our knock was followed by the welcome jingle

Of her approaching step,
Evoking Christmas spirit much as church bells did.

Sane, sensible, adored,
Deserving lady—how I envied her!
Never before or after have I laid eyes
On anything I coveted so much.
I secretly enquired the name
Of a store which would retail
Such wonders, but was afraid to go,
Knowing the clerk would say,
"But madam these slippers may be sold
Only as gifts!" Knowing I would never be
A woman for whom anyone would buy
Black velvet slippers with golden bells.

Once the guests were gathered in the living room, where the chairs had been pushed back toward the walls, Mother supervised party games that everyone, young and old, could play together. One was musical chairs. The one person left in a chair at the end was the winner and received a prize. Another game involved passing a secret around the circle. Two people seated beside each other were given the same sentence, which each whispered to his neighbor. When the secret met halfway around the circle, the last two to hear it repeated aloud what they were told. The two sentences were never the same—and neither was the original sentence. I expect having us little children in the circle added some interesting twists.

The guests then mingled in the dining room for Christmas candies, cookies, and cakes. The dining room table was covered with a red cloth. In the center among sprays of cedar and pine, a shiny, red glass Santa Claus nestled into his sleigh, pulled by eight white reindeer. Frederick and I spent hours trying to fashion a harness for these reindeer from string or ribbon. That's why two of them now have only one antler.

The highlight of the evening came when the guests were again settled in the living room: Mother would read Clement Moore's *The Night Before Christmas*. Children's eyes were wide with magic expectation—yes, "visions of sugar plums" swam in *our* heads. Finally, Mother stood at the door holding a basket of small gifts, from which each departing guest selected one: an ornament, a yo-yo, a tiny notebook, or a pencil.

At bedtime, Frederick and I and, in later years, Byron, hung our stockings from hooks on the mantel. Daddy's cousin, Julian Coffee, made a stocking for each of us for our first Christmas. Orion told us her husband's father and friends had owned a general store called Free, Coffee & Bacon—their family names. Our stockings were made of white flannel with red heel, toe, and trim around the top. The heel and toe were edged with green stitching and our names were embroidered in red below the top band. At some point, Mother and I made Daddy a matching stocking, but of red-and-white striped flannel. One Christmas when Grandmother came to spend Christmas with us, she brought a stocking for Mother, suggesting we fill it for her. She had noticed we gave Mother little for Christmas, as she handled the shopping. Grandmother had brought Jergens lotion, SweetHeart soap, notepaper, and Mr. Goodbars for us to fill the red net stocking. Grandmother had a special and thoughtful knack for gift-giving. Mother used that stocking for years. Even after I made one for her modeled after ours, we put it inside the red net one Grandmother had brought. And every year for the rest of her life, Santa left Mr. Goodbars in her stocking.

After putting a plate of cookies for Santa Claus on a hassock near the fireplace, we warmed our flannel blankets before the fire and reluctantly crawled into bed, wrapping our feet in the blankets. "Are you sure those coals aren't so hot he'll get burned?" Frederick asked. We lay there, worried that Mother would not go to bed in time for Santa Claus to come. In spite of our efforts to stay awake, we eventually fell asleep. One year Frederick woke in the night and actually heard the "prancing and pawing of each little hoof" on the roof!

I remember the minute: I was seven years old, visiting Nana. She had invited a Darien girl about my age to spend the day with me. As she and I climbed the stairs that day, she said, "You know Santa Claus isn't real." Although this disappointed me then, I now know with certainty that she was wrong—he still fills my stocking every year.

Christmas Gift!

Finally, Christmas dawned! "Christmas gift! Christmas gift!" We each tried to be first to say these words. Later, when I wondered what the phrase could mean, I asked Mother. She told us that it originated in the days of slavery. Some plantation owners allowed their slaves a little more freedom on Christmas Day. On some holdings, the slaves began the day with a dancing march to the master's house, beating makeshift drums and singing. When they reached the Big House, the children would shout out, "Christmas gift!" Often material gifts were distributed on that day: the year's worth of clothing or some food delicacy.

We never rushed to our stockings on Christmas morning. There were rules: *everyone* had to be dressed before *anyone* could go into the living room. The one exception was that Daddy went in to light the fire "without looking at anything." Oh, the magic of the first sight of the treasures Santa Claus had left! It was truly miraculous that such wonders could appear—that Santa Claus could come silently down the chimney with exactly the gifts we wanted. Our stockings were stuffed and toys were placed in "our" chairs beside the fireplace. There was always a doll for me. After the baby-doll years, Santa brought Madame Alexander dolls: particularly Carolyn, who was actually Alice in Wonderland; and Cissy, in a long-waisted navy taffeta dress, straw hat, and high-heeled shoes. Orion said Cissy looked "just like a lady you'd see on Peachtree Street in Atlanta."

Frederick's gifts in various years were a farm set, including a metal barn, plastic fences, and farm animals; sets of bowlegged cowboys and Indians, who sat comfortably astride their horses;

Lincoln logs, from which we built log houses; an Erector Set, which included perforated metal strips, with screws and nuts to assemble them. One year, Santa brought both of us cap pistols with holsters, and cowboy hats. The pistols came with little red rolls of caps. When they were properly loaded, the metal guns shot realistically, leaving a lingering smell of sulfur. There were books for each of us—and disappointingly, some new underwear.

Out of our stockings we pulled nuts, oranges, and silver tips, which we were supposed not to eat until after breakfast. We always managed to sneak a few into our mouths. And at the bottom of each of our stockings every year was a sterling silver demitasse spoon. Many of these commemorated local or historic places: Chippewa Square in Savannah, Mount Vernon, Williamsburg, Monticello. Some were decorated with Christmas designs: holly and berries, Santa with a pack of toys atop a chimney—and I still have mine.

Though we stared longingly at the wrapped packages under the tree, Mother called us to the dining room for breakfast. Orion joined us in time for a treat of cinnamon rolls, scrambled eggs, and venison sausage—not our usual fare.

Finally, it was time to open the gifts under the tree. Daddy picked up each one and read the name on the tag. Among my gifts were doll clothes Nana had made. How did she know which doll Santa was bringing? One year Mrs. Taylor made bridal gowns with net veils for Dianne's and my dolls. Daddy usually gave Mother Royal Secret perfume, while she tended to handkerchiefs for him. One year, she gave him a small sterling silver pill box, which he carried in his pocket. He always had a handful of pills to take.

Christmas dinner followed, including a large turkey. Mother always got up well before breakfast to put this bird in the oven. Somehow, it never seemed to be completely done in time for dinner, which was our midday meal; the evening meal was supper. Daddy sliced off enough pieces of the turkey for our dinner and the rest went back into the oven. Mother cooked English peas with pearl onions, ground up her special cranberry-orange relish in the meat grinder, and made cornbread dressing with lots of sausage balls on top—to this day my favorite part of Christmas (or Thanksgiving) dinner. Sometimes, if we had company with us, Mother cooked oyster stew. It took me a long time to acquire a taste for that dish. Daddy peeled dozens of oranges for ambrosia. Wearing a bibbed apron tied high above his waist, he could peel an entire skin in one long strip, which fell into the white enamel dishpan. With the ambrosia, we had Grandmother's light fruitcake and her special pound cake.

During the afternoon, Daddy or Mr. Taylor would go by boat to pick up a minister at Buckingham Landing, who conducted a Christmas service in the Honey Horn Chapel. Often some or all three of our grandparents came over on the same trip as well to spend the night and prolong the Christmas celebration. If we were "lucky" enough to have cold weather, the chapel could be frigid. It was heated by a single gas space heater—and not insulated!

Before bedtime, Mother sat us down to begin writing thank-you letters.

Turkeys at Church

Frank Harrington, at Peachtree Presbyterian Church in Atlanta, would say after he baptized an infant, "I pray there will never be a time in your life when you do not know the love of Jesus Christ." I am blessed to have lived that life. From my earliest memories I have known that God loves me. I know my abiding trust in God was nurtured by the loving family into which I was born: I was the first child, the first grandchild, and the first niece or nephew for two aunts and two uncles—in addition to being an adorable, chubby little girl.

Mother and Daddy taught us early to kneel and to "say our prayers," praying with us at bedtime:

> *Now I lay me down to sleep;*
> *I pray Thee, Lord, my soul to keep.*
> *If I should die before I wake,*
> *I pray Thee, Lord, my soul to take.*

I still consider this a good bedtime prayer. Mother and Daddy knelt beside their bed each night to say their prayers. I also saw Grandmother, Nana, and Grandfather do the same—powerful witnesses.

In our early days, in Hinesville, Mother and Daddy took Frederick and me to Sunday School at the Flemington Presbyterian Church. Miss Eliza and Miss Josie were the teachers, but I don't remember any of the other children—nor my "Sunday best" clothes. As we got in the car for the short drive to Flemington, Daddy put a nickel in my hand and said, "Now, put this in the collection."

I asked, "How does the money get to God?"

Mother said, "The Church uses it to do things that God wants done."

Much later when we were given a weekly allowance of $2.25, we were expected to give $0.25 to the church, our tithe—a discipline for life.

My lullabies were hymns—good ole Methodist and Baptist ones. In my mind I hear them in various voices, in various places.

> *Sing them over again to me,*
> *Wonderful words of life.*
> *Let me more of their beauty see,*
> *Wonderful words of life.*

This in Nana's whispery, barely audible voice as she cuddled me in her small lap, singing me to sleep. The little black wicker rocking chair in the upstairs bedroom at the Ridge creaked an accompaniment. Sometimes the words faded into a low, breathy whistle. Nana's face was peaceful and her eyes smiled. Her lips were thin. She sang comforting words:

> *There is a name I love to hear;*
> *I love to sing its worth. . . .*
> *Oh, how I love Jesus! . . .*
> *The sweetest name on earth.*

Or on a livelier note:

> *Give me that old time religion. . . .*
> *It was good for Paul and Silas,*
> *And it's good enough for me!*

In Hinesville, Mother sat in her black rocker in the hall, near the oil heater. Her rocker was larger, but it too creaked. She sang:

> *Bring them in! Bring them in!*

> *Bring them in from the fields of sin.*
> *Bring them in! Bring them in!*
> *Bring the wandering ones to Jesus!*

Or:

> *I was sinking deep in sin, far from the peaceful shore,*
> *When the master of the sea heard my despairing cry,*
> *From the waters lifted me—now safe am I.*
> *Love lifted me. Love lifted me.*
> *When nothing else could help, love lifted me.*

Or another time:

> *On a hill far away, stood an old rugged cross,*
> *The emblem of suffering and shame.*

And I clearly saw the cross, on a little mound, fixed on one of the colorful braided rag rugs Nana made!

Mother and Nana both varied the religious routine with traditional favorites:

> *My bonnie lies over the ocean.*
> *My bonnie lies over the sea.*
> *My bonnie lies over the ocean.*
> *Oh, bring back my bonnie to me.*

As we saw the moon through Frederick's and my high bedroom window of the apartment:

> *I see the moon. The moon sees me,*
> *Down through the leaves of the old oak tree.*
> *God bless the moon. And God bless me.*
> *And God bless the one that I long to see.*

There were also the confusing Christmas carols. For example, hearing "Silent Night," I assumed that "round yon virgin" was something like "around the corner."

When we moved to Hilton Head Island, where there was no Sunday School, Mother taught us at home. On Sunday mornings, she read to us from *Hurlbut's Story of the Bible*. This is a beautiful Bible story book, following the Bible narrative closely, written in words a child understands. The illustrations are classical paintings, which bring the stories to life. *Hurlbut's* served me well when I was teaching second-grade Sunday School years later in Atlanta. I have passed this book on to my great-nephew for a new generation to enjoy. As other children moved to Honey Horn, they joined our class—first Dianne, then Bernadette. Wherever Mother saw a need, she filled it—quietly.

Though in 1950 there was no church for white residents, there were a number of active black churches. Services rotated among them, as there was not a regular preacher at each. I remember lying in bed on a Sunday night (and sometimes on other nights) and hearing drumbeats from the church across the creek. The sound sank into my chest, an African rhythm. I pictured the swaying congregation praising God from their hearts. Is this one reason why from my first visit to Kenya, I have felt it is my "soul country"?

Praise houses survived from plantation days. Once Daddy took us into one, a small plank building with a few backless benches. In these praise houses, small groups gathered between regular services to sing and praise God. David Reese's evocative painting of a praise house, which hangs in my home now, colors my memory. This painting was one of a series commissioned for the January 1956 issue of *Ford Times* magazine. Other paintings in the series included the Baynard Ruins, the Honey Horn Big House, a shell ring, bateaus at Paddy's Camp with nets drying, and the steam cannon.

In 1953, Daddy decided the white residents needed an organized church. He arranged for an Episcopal priest, Mr. Haynesworth, to come to the Island periodically to lead services

A Praise House *(painting by David Reese, 1956)*.

in the one-room chapel at Honey Horn Plantation. In the afternoon, after Mr. Haynesworth had led services at the Church of the Cross in Bluffton, Daddy met him at Buckingham Landing and brought him over by boat. After the first February service, Mother wrote in her diary, "Fred says, 'Maybe it's good we begin with a "foreign" religion'"—he meant it was not Presbyterian! Five rows of pews provided seating for fifty people. Actually, these were plain wooden chairs with folding seats and shared armrests. On a slightly raised platform at the front was a sturdy, wooden lectern, supporting a large, leather-bound pulpit Bible. A pump organ stood to the side. In the early years, there was often no one to play it.

When I was in fifth grade, Dianne and I began taking piano lessons in Bluffton. After Nana had heard us play in an early recital, she said to me, "You must keep practicing your hymns. You never know when someone will want to sing and will ask if anyone can play the piano." And, lo and behold, the time came when our fledgling church in the chapel at Honey Horn was without an organist. Dianne and I played the pump organ, knowing nothing about playing an organ. For the preludes, we learned different hymns from the *Broadman Hymnal*, such as "He Leadeth Me" and "Just as I Am." As much as I love the song, I never mastered "Blessed Assurance"!

In 1957, the First Presbyterian Church of Hilton Head Island was founded in the chapel. The organizing minister was young Mills Peebles. He and his wife moved to the Island with their infant son and lived in the small house beyond Miss Milley's. Frederick and I went to confirmation classes on his screened front porch and made our affirmations of faith on the organizational Sunday. Daddy was determined we be among the seventeen charter members. Others were Mother, Daddy, Orion, Grandmother, Phyllis Stone (a "cradle Episcopalian," and Daddy's longtime secretary), Charles Fraser, and Pete McGinty.[3]

---

[3] Completing the roster were Frank and Leone Free, cousins of Daddy's; Mary Alice and Carroll Sydney Hendry, The Hilton Head Company accountant; Alva Hines; E. W. Horton; Robert Weldy; and Mrs. Joyce Weldy, who served for years as organist for the congregation.

(His wife, Aileen, never made the change from the Episcopal Church.) Mother then began teaching the church Sunday School, in a room upstairs in the Jumper Barn, where the Dixons had lived. She taught Sunday School for the next thirty-five years.

On either side of the chapel were the dog kennels and the turkey roost. So worship was often accompanied by cows munching, turkeys gobbling and clucking in the yard, and a canine choir from the kennels. The turkey flock would fly over the fence into the churchyard and be unable to find their way back out, even with the gate opened. One duty of the ushers was to try to keep turkeys off the cars, though they could do nothing about the barking dogs.

One summer, Frederick, Dianne, and I attended Vacation Bible School at the Episcopal Church of the Cross in Bluffton. Mother and Mrs. Taylor took turns taking us over on the ferry. Frederick, the other younger children, and I learned "Stand Up, Stand Up for Jesus," while Dianne's older group learned "All Hail the Power of Jesus' Name." We each built a church sanctuary in a

The Honey Horn Chapel.

Turkeys with the dog kennel behind, right, and storage shed.

shoe box, including a baptismal font which we molded from clay. In my Presbyterian heritage, there were no baptismal fonts. Our heads were sprinkled from a bowl of water. In fact, my family had a small crystal bowl used at each of our baptisms. On the ride back to the Island, we sang both the hymns we had learned.

Daddy as Doctor

Caring for the sick and injured was second nature to Daddy, the son of a doctor. He had listened to Dr. Hack discuss his patients and sometimes watched his father treat them. So when Daddy came to Hilton Head Island, where there was no doctor nor any type of medical clinic, he stepped into the void. In the earliest years, there were no telephones, so he sometimes could not even consult a doctor quickly. In a serious emergency, he could use the short-wave radio, installed in our dining room, to reach a doctor in Savannah or Bluffton, who was flown to the Island. Mother wrote in her diary of a doctor being flown over once for one of the hunters at the Big House, who had become ill. But if a man had been injured working in a sawmill at the South End, waiting for a doctor to arrive would have taken a long time. Often, Daddy was "the doctor."

He doctored our family with a thermometer and a few basic medicines. For fever and minor pains, Mother gave us aspirin crushed in a teaspoon of white Karo syrup. For sore throat or other infections, Daddy gave us Terramycin, which was a pink antibiotic, with an unpleasant, medicinal cherry flavor. For an upset stomach or diarrhea, he dosed us with paregoric, a narcotic containing opium, I've since learned. But it tasted good. My strongest memory of paregoric is Mother giving it to us for an attack of Montezuma's revenge in Monterrey, Mexico, some years later. Stumped toes, scraped knees, and oyster shell cuts were cleaned with hydrogen peroxide, which foamed as it "killed the germs." After treating them with red Mercurochrome—or in worse cases with stinging Merthiolate—Mother covered these wounds with white fabric Band-Aids. When a crab pinched my heel, Daddy had me soak it in boric acid. The itching of tick and red bug bites was lessened by soaking in a tub of warm water with boric acid. I think red bugs are the same as chiggers. They lived primarily in Spanish moss.

The only serious family illness Daddy diagnosed and monitored, aside from his own hypertension, was Frederick's diabetes. When Frederick was six years old, Daddy recognized what his often being tired, hungry, and thirsty but not gaining weight might mean, and took him to Dr. Waring, our pediatrician, in Savannah. Frederick was in Telfair Hospital for several days while doctors monitored his progress, prescribed daily insulin injections, and designed a diet to help control the condition. The whole family followed his diet: lean meat, vegetables, virtually no bread, and no sugar. Well, Mother gave the rest of us sweet desserts, but she made sugar-free Jell-O and baked custard for Frederick. Vegetables were classified into three categories, based on carbohydrate content. The amount allowed depended on this classification.

Interestingly, this pediatrician Dr. Waring was an amateur expert on Indian settlements along the Atlantic coast—an interest he had developed in his youth. He spent much time on the Island studying the shell rings, pottery shards, and arrowheads found in abundance all over the Island. Many artifacts were uncovered every time fields were plowed. He identified the remains of settlements which he dated as early as 2000 BC.

Sometimes Daddy was called on to treat more serious injuries. For the men who worked in the sawmills or on fishing boats, Daddy stabilized broken bones and bandaged finger stumps (and the severed fingers) until the patients could be transferred to a hospital on the mainland. He must have had morphine or some other painkiller to use in these situations. The worst injury I recall personally seeing was Mr. Sconyers' burned back. The Sconyers built one of the first weekend beach houses at North Forest Beach. The house was raised on concrete columns, a building style which is returning, with modifications, as sea levels rise. Mr. Sconyers

Daddy as Doctor

had been helping a neighbor who was roofing his house. As he carried a bucket of hot tar up a ladder, he slipped and the tar splattered onto his shoulders and chest. His friends drove him to Honey Horn, where Daddy smeared lots of butter over the burned areas (with the tar still attached!). He bandaged him in voluminous white bedsheets, following a doctor's instructions over the car phone. By this time, Daddy had replaced the two-way radio with a mobile telephone, installed in his car, which allowed him to reach a doctor in an emergency. To be near the phone, Mr. Sconyers was treated in the car, in the shade of the big cedar tree between our house and the Taylors'. The phone reception was better in the field, too. As soon as possible, he was ferried to the mainland to a doctor.

The "car phone" Daddy had was not unlike a two-way radio. It had a receiver like a normal telephone, but the speaker had to depress a bar in the receiver to be heard. He had to release it quickly to hear the response.

Frederick recalls that Daddy also gave penicillin shots to men and animals of all sizes—the miracle drug. I'm sure that recognizing the situation on the Island, Daddy's doctor in Savannah supplied him with these prescription medicines so he could administer extended first aid.

As we were growing up, I wasn't struck with how unusual it was to live where there was no medical care. Since our arrival on the Island, there had never been a doctor nearby. Daddy, like Mother, stepped in and filled needs as he saw them. Though Daddy wasn't a doctor and I never heard anyone call him "Dr. Hack," he had followed in his father's footsteps.

Hurricane's Coming!

Daddy stands on the beach watching the waves. Bracing himself against the rising wind, he times their frequency, estimates their height. The longer the space between, the larger the waves—and the closer the storm is. The wind drives the rain against his body. He wears an old felt hat, a mid-thigh heavy army jacket, khaki pants, and hunting boots, dark brown from many coats of saddle soap.

He watches the waves at Folly Field, then drives farther south to check the ocean—riding out the plantation road at the North Carolina Hunting Club. Then he returns to Jenkins Island to check the water level. There is a tide gauge attached to one of the creosoted posts of the dock. By walking down the ferry loading ramp, he has a clear view.

Back in the car, he calls the National Weather Service on the mobile phone to report his observations. Based on his and other observations, the location, severity, and direction of the storm are being plotted.

Returning home, Daddy tells Mother what he's seen. "Hazel's heading our way. It's time to evacuate." He goes back to the car to use the phone to call Mose Hudson, the ferry captain, on the mainland. "Mose, the hurricane's coming our way. The waves are already twelve feet high and breaking every thirty seconds. Let's get the ferry on over and take people off."

Daddy, Mr. Taylor, and Fuskie have taken Mother's car and the Taylors' to the ferry landing and left them in line. There were already a couple of other cars lined up. Others are notified of the evacuation. Nine cars can leave on the ferry. The weather might or might not allow a second trip.

We children are up now, getting dressed, excited to be wakened before dawn. There is a sense of danger in the air, but we aren't afraid. Daddy will take care of us. Grandmother is with us on a visit. Mrs. Stone drives to our house from Folly Field. Mother packs a few clothes for us and collects her silver chest and a few other valuable items, and loads them in the car.

Almost jumping with excitement, we plead, "Mother, can't we stay and see the storm? Maybe it won't be bad."

"Daddy will be busy taking care of other things. He doesn't need to worry about us, too."

"How high will the water come? Will it be in the house?"

"I don't know. It's already at the top of the gauge in the creek." In our house are small, round holes in the floor, every few feet along the walls. They had been drilled to let water out after the hurricane of 1936 (or was it 1947?), when water had, indeed, risen into the Honey Horn houses.

In the dark, not yet daybreak, Mother bundles us into the car and drives to Jenkins Island. In the lane, we pass dump trucks and other equipment being moved to our front field, one of the highest open areas on the Island. When we reach the dock, there are enough cars lined up to fill two ferries. Some people at the front of the line are making room in their cars for others; our car is full. We transfer our little bit of luggage. Mrs. Stone has brought her "valuables" in two paper bags. When the ferry arrives, Mr. Hudson loads the cars in a driving rain, and the ferry sets off for a rolling ride to Buckingham Landing. Mother drives through Savannah to Grandmother's house in Flemington. When we arrive and unload the car, Mrs. Stone realizes one of the bags she has brought holds her garbage! She'd intended to drop it at the garbage dump on the way to our house.

Daddy stayed on the Island. He, Mr. Pat, Mr. Taylor, Fuskie, and others kept an eye on things and continued to report to the

National Weather Service. There were other trucks and equipment to move to high ground, animals to be sheltered in the barn. The men needed to be there if windows had to be boarded up. Or did they just enjoy the excitement of the storm—without their families to worry about?

Hazel made landfall in North Carolina, October 15, 1954. Our Island was again spared. It had been another stormy birthday for Frederick, now seven years old.

Daddy routinely sent us off the Island when Atlantic hurricanes threatened. Hurricane Able had made landfall in Beaufort in August 1952. Several threatened in 1953, apparently causing some damage on Hilton Head Island. Mother noted in her diary that several boats, which had sunk at Jenkins Island, had been raised and were running again.

We lived with the weather in those days before air conditioning and central heating. Daddy, especially, suffered from the summer heat. He slept in his underwear with an electric fan blowing at high speed across his body. There were nights when I dampened my pajamas before putting them on, in hopes that evaporation would cool me and let me sleep. Afternoon naps served not just to ward off polio, but to keep us out of the day's most burning heat. "Only mad dogs and Englishmen go out in the midday sun."

In winter, our heat sources were the fireplace in the living room, the wood stove in the kitchen, and propane gas space heaters. The heaters sat in each room on asbestos-backed metal pads, which protected the floor. Each morning we hopped out of bed and ran to the heater, which Daddy lit before waking us. Amazingly, I don't recall any of us being burned by backing into one of the heaters as we tried to warm our backsides. Nor do I remember any of the deerskin rugs in front of each heater catching fire though these hides still had hair on them. One winter Mother woke us in the middle of the night to see snow falling. By morning, it was completely gone.

Mother, at the weather station, receiving National Weather Service Institutional Award from Earl Ramsey, 1981 (photo courtesy of The Island Packet*).*

Not only did we live with the weather, we recorded it. In 1953, as an extension of Daddy's storm-watching, the National Weather Bureau installed an official weather-monitoring station in the field near our house. Each afternoon, Daddy or Mother recorded the readings for temperature and precipitation. A large copper tube, with a wide mouth forming a funnel, caught rain, which they measured—to the hundredth of an inch—by inserting a slim, calibrated wooden stick into it. Two thermometers were housed in a louvred, white, wooden box raised on three-foot legs. One was a red alcohol thermometer which read the current temperature. There was a bead suspended in it to mark the lowest temperature. A silver mercury thermometer recorded the highest temperature. After the reading for the day was recorded, the thermometers were released from the horizontal position and spun to force the mercury back into the reservoir. Daily recordings were made of the high, low, and current temperature readings, and type and amount of precipitation. Always rain for Hilton Head Island!

Later, the Weather Service erected a wind gauge in the front field. Data were transmitted to a machine in the house, where a delicately balanced pen recorded wind direction and speed on a cylindrical graph. Situating the paper roll and refilling the ink reservoir were frustrating. Byron recorded the final weather reading on the day Mother died in 1998. The National Weather Service presented an award to Mother in 1981 for twenty-five years of service, though that was twenty-eight years after she and Daddy began monitoring the weather. The Weather Service presented a second award for Mother and Daddy's more than forty-five years of faithful service. Unfortunately, this recognition came posthumously for them both. Recording daily weather is a habit I have not been able to shake. After my death, someone will find notebooks filled with daily readings for every day we have been in Highlands—along with a record of the birds seen near our house each week.

Sunrise

In 1950, when Daddy and his associates formed The Hilton Head Company and purchased more than eight thousand acres on Hilton Head Island, change accelerated. As children, we didn't notice what was happening. After a couple of years we had electricity, a washing machine, and a freezer. Ferry service began in 1953, bringing more cars, truck farming, better access to building materials, and eventually tourists. A few houses were built at Forest Beach by adventurous souls.

In 1953, the McIntosh family had built twenty beach cottages, raised on concrete block pillars, at Folly Field. Daddy called this development "the one that built the bridge." It was a major factor in convincing the State to construct the bridge to the Island. In 1955, State Representative Wilton Graves had opened the first motel, the Sea Crest, which consisted of two guest rooms built of concrete blocks, on the beach near Coligny Circle. Some of the earliest visitors were flown over by private planes, which landed on the beach. In 1956, Norris and Lois Richardson opened the Island's first supermarket and were founders of the First Baptist Church.

Increasing development led to the formation of the Hilton Head Island Toll Bridge Authority, charged with planning and overseeing construction of a bridge to the Island. Its members were John M. Sturgeon, chairman; G. G. Dowling, counsel; Fred C. Hack, secretary; and Captain C. C. Moses. On May 19, 1956, Armed Forces Day, the James F. Byrnes Crossing, a drawbridge, was opened and dedicated. A celebration in the field at Honey Horn Plantation marked the opening. Mother wore a new green linen dress with matching straw hat and sling-back pumps. *The*

State newspaper on May 20, 1956, described the event. It included a seventeen-gun salute to former Governor Byrnes; jet aircraft and a dirigible overhead; an address by Donald S. Russell, president of the University of South Carolina; and a response by Governor Byrnes. These and other dignitaries, including General Mark Clark, president of The Citadel, and Lt. Governor Fritz Hollings, reviewed the troops: units from most branches of service plus The Citadel. Following a picnic on the grounds, the John Sturgeon family hosted a reception at Rose Hill, a property they owned near Bluffton.

Earlier, on May 5, *The State* newspaper had reported, "Churchill Is Invited to Attend Dedication of 'Byrnes Crossing.'" Mr. Dowling, who had been born in England, had delivered the invitation to Mr. Churchill. Sadly, the former prime minister did not attend.

Fittingly, Mose Hudson continued to supervise passage to the Island. He manned the drawbridge, collecting tolls of $2.50 to drive onto the Island; driving off was free. He also swung the bridge open for larger boats on Skull Creek to pass through. As these boats approached the bridge, they blew their deep whistles. As we heard that haunting sound in the night, we had no idea how completely our world had changed.

Epilogue

When Frederick had written for the *Hilton Head School News* in April of 1956, "On April 2, Daddy, Byron and I rode over the bridge to Pinkney [sic] Island," I'm sure none of us could have imagined how quickly our Island paradise would be altered. In fact, the change had begun in 1950, when Daddy and Mother moved to Honey Horn Plantation and their characters began to mold the future development of the community. By the time I was in high school, I had mixed feelings about development of the Island. It was Daddy's livelihood and his dream, and he planned with care for the environment, but it was taking away the parts of Hilton Head Island I treasured most: the woods, wildlife, deserted beaches, oyster-shelled roads, marsh tackies passing in the night, long horseback rides in the woods. While writing these tales from my past, I have recognized anew how my life was shaped by the time spent on the Island at the dawn of the modern era.

The gates were opened and change came quickly. One of the first people to cross the bridge was Charles E. Fraser, youngest son of General Fraser. He had worked on the Island in the summers while he was in college and was now full of ambitious plans for the development of what became Sea Pines Plantation. Daddy and The Hilton Head Company continued the planning of Forest Beach development, where he designed and named the first traffic circle on the Island, Coligny Circle. He named the streets in South Forest Beach for local birds, in alphabetical order, which made it easier to find streets. The Company continued development on the northern sections of the Island: Port Royal, Grasslawn, and Shipyard Plantations. In 1971, The Hilton Head Company was sold and Daddy entered an uneasy retirement. He and Mother lived at Honey Horn for the rest of their lives.

Daddy died in February 1978. He had come with a dream and worked the remainder of his life to realize his vision for the Island. As a child, I had no idea how he was able to convince businessmen to finance his plans for the Island. More than a developer, he worked on countless projects to make Hilton Head Island a better place to live. These included being a founding elder of the First Presbyterian Church; serving as secretary of the Hilton Head Island Toll Bridge Authority; donating land (personally or with associates through his various companies) for the fire lookout tower, several successive airport locations, the public library, The Children's Center, the first fire station, several churches, and other organizations.

After Daddy's death, we heard stories from Islanders whom he had helped without our knowing it. Byron learned from a Native Islander that, during the time Thorne and Loomis owned Honey Horn Plantation, their overseer had bought up parcels of land owned by black people, which were sold for unpaid taxes. When Daddy's company purchased that land, he allowed these prior owners to redeem the land they had lost earlier. Sometimes he simply offered a needed word of encouragement. In the 1990s, when a woman realized Byron was Fred Hack's son, she told him that years before she had been in a fender bender on the highway. Daddy was among those who stopped to check on her. She was upset that her husband would be angry with her for the damage to the car. Daddy pulled a silver dollar from his pocket and gave it to her. "No, he won't. He'll just be happy you were not hurt." She still had the silver dollar. Daddy was one of the four initial inductees into the Hilton Head Island Hall of Fame in 2012. Others inducted that year were Charles Fraser; Charlotte Heinrichs, who did much charitable work, particularly in helping Native Islanders access clean water; and Charlie Simmons, the original provider of transportation to the Island.

Mother was a strong leader in Island life, shunning praise and

Epilogue

credit for what she did. In her acceptance of the Alice Glenn Doughtie Good Citizenship Award in 1992, she said, "All these people come here after their exciting accomplishments and travel, and all I can say is, 'I stayed here and raised my children.'" When she died in 1998 at eighty-three, she left a remarkable legacy. In 1953, she and Orion founded a publishing company to publish the first modern history of the Island, *A Sea Island Chronicle*, written by Virginia C. Holmgren. She was instrumental in founding the Hilton Head Island Branch Library; the Hilton Head Island Women's Association, of which she was the first president; and The Children's Center, which still provides affordable daycare for children of working mothers. She and Daddy were the founders of the First Presbyterian Church. Mother and two other Presbyterian ladies opened a small thrift store in 1965 and named it the Bargain Box. It became an Island fixture, where more than 250 volunteers now find a bond of camaraderie. In its more than fifty years of existence, the Bargain Box has donated more than $13 million to numerous other nonprofit organizations in the community. In 2013, Mother was inducted into the Hilton Head Island Hall of Fame.

Mother and Daddy were in the right place at the right time and had a unique opportunity to help shape the development and character of an area, which to this day reflects their values: their commitment to faith, the natural environment, and service to the community. Modern Hilton Head Island began to emerge the day Daddy and Mother moved their young family to the Island and committed the rest of their lives to the Island community.

Frederick, with his wife, Carol, is the only major player from these memories who still lives on the Island. He worked with Daddy at The Hilton Head Company in the last years before Daddy's retirement. After leaving for Agnes Scott College in 1963, I returned to the Island for only a few summers. Byron and his wife, Debby, cared for Mother until her death, then moved from the Island. Dianne Taylor married Ashley Bush in the chapel at Honey Horn Plantation in July 1962—during a hurricane, which almost kept the groom from the wedding. They moved from the Island. Sadly, my dear friend, Sylvia Dianne Taylor Bush, passed away on May 12, 2018. Orion, Dellie and Fuskie Simmons, Aileen and Pete McGinty have all passed away. Frederick, Byron, and I are the keepers of our history and heritage.

When the State Highway Department decided in 1989 that a parkway should be constructed to carry traffic more directly to the south end of the Island, planners determined the best route was directly through the middle of Honey Horn Plantation. The State condemned the property for the right-of-way. When construction began, the old entrance to the Plantation was closed off and a new one was opened, leading under the parkway.

In two separate transactions, my family sold the now divided portions of the Plantation to the town of Hilton Head Island. The eastern portion was sold first. In an effort to preserve green spaces on the Island, the town created Jarvis Park, left largely in its natural state. A few months after Mother's death in 1998, Frederick and Byron began further negotiations with the town, resulting in the sale of the remaining parcel of land. The town leased the land and buildings to the Coastal Discovery Museum, which, in 2007, moved their headquarters to Honey Horn Plantation. Our family's main concern in the sale and transfer was that the Big House be preserved. Though the Highway Department's condemnation of the property for the right-of-way for the parkway was sad, this later sale was satisfying to me because it meant some of the old buildings would be preserved and their history shared with the public.

These buildings remaining at Honey Horn Plantation are among the few locations on the Island which are recognizable from my childhood. In 1957, the Highway Department relocated Spanish Wells Road so it no longer passes through the Plantation, but the wooden bridge was not removed until sometime in the 1960s. The original structure of the Big House is one of the two oldest structures remaining on the Island, the other being Baynard Mausoleum located at Zion Cemetery at the tip of Broad Creek.

Epilogue

The Museum's exhibit halls and a gift shop occupy the Big House, known now as the Discovery House. To create a large hall, the two bedrooms opposite the living room were combined and the bathrooms removed. I regret that those magnificent bathrooms were not preserved to show the way of life for the visiting hunters.

Most of the Armstrongs' house, now named the Supervisor's House, was demolished, including the apartment where the Thompsons lived. The remaining space serves as the Discovery Lab. The house where we lived is used for offices and storage, and is designated the Armstrong-Hack House. The Honey Horn Chapel was moved to the campus of the First Presbyterian Church on Highway 278, before the parkway was built. The Big Barn had burned in 1963 and the tack room a few years later. The Jumper Barn at the far end of the field, now simply the Horse Barn, remains. A couple of marsh tackies are on loan to the museum and are stabled there—a true part of living history. The dog kennels and turkey roost are long gone. The one-room schoolhouse was purchased and moved to another location and finally to the mainland. We then lost track of its whereabouts.

Dawn has passed. The sun has risen on the modern Hilton Head Island. But the memories are precious.

Acknowledgments

Without attending Linda Hobson's class on "Writing Your Memoir" in 2007, I would not have known how to begin this project. Special thanks go to Judy Goldman, author and memoirist, who edited this manuscript and provided valuable guidance and encouragement. Thanks also to several friends who have read my manuscript and made helpful suggestions: Janet Allen, early in the process; Diane Cox McPhail, friend and novelist; my cousin, Kit Stebbins Sutherland; friends Becky Bryson and Helen Moore. Several friends who have recently published their own books have been generous in offering advice from their experiences. Extra efforts were made by my two brothers, Frederick and Byron Hack, who have read the manuscript several times, fact-checking me, providing documentation, and helping refresh my memories. My dear husband, Gerry, not only has read and reread the book but also has gracefully endured my moods and the time I have devoted to this project.

The majority of the photographs were taken contemporaneously by my family, using their Kodak Brownie cameras. *The Island Packet* granted permission for me to use one of their photographs. Kevin Vinson of High Country Photo in Highlands, North Carolina, produced the digital form of all the photographs. Hank Ross, owner of Ross Landscape Architecture in Highlands, produced, mostly from my memories, the historic map of Honey Horn Plantation, showing the location of buildings from my childhood.

Brief Chronology

February 16, 1914 – Daddy, Frederick Courtland Hack, born
May 14, 1915 – Mother, Will Davis Stebbins, born
March 28, 1942 – Mother and Daddy married
July 13, 1945 – Martha Avary Hack born
October 12, 1947 – Frederick Courtland Hack, Jr., born
June 1950 – Hack family moved to Hilton Head Island
September 1951 – My first day of school
April 7, 1952 – Orion Byron Hack born
1953 – Ferry service begun to Hilton Head Island; twenty raised cottages built at Folly Field
1955 – J. Wilton Graves opened the Sea Crest Motel
May 19, 1956 – James F. Byrnes Crossing opened
January 10, 1978 – Daddy's death
March 5, 1998 – Mother's death

Sources and Inspiration

Coastal Discovery Museum, Natalie Harvey, editor. *Hilton Head Island*. Images of America. Charleston, SC: Arcadia Publishing, 1998.

Compton's Pictured Encyclopedia. Chicago: F. E. Compton & Company, 1922.

Conant, Jennet. *Tuxedo Park: A Wall Street Tycoon and the Secret Palace of Science That Changed the Course of World War II*. New York: Simon & Schuster, 2002.

Cross, Wilbur. *First Presbyterian Church, Hilton Head Island, South Carolina: The Authorized History of a Dynamic Community Church*. Franklin, TN: Providence House Publishers, 1994.

Danielson, Michael N. *Profits and Politics in Paradise: The Development of Hilton Head Island*. Columbia: University of South Carolina Press, 1995.

Dinesen, Isak. *Out of Africa*. New York: Random House, Inc., 1937.

Golden Book of Favorite Songs: A Treasury of the Best Songs of Our People. Chicago: Hall & McCreary Company, 1946.

Gray, William S., A. Sterl Artley, May Hill Arbuthnot. *The New We Look and See*. The New Basic Readers. Chicago: Scott, Foresman and Company, 1951.

Hack, Billie S., diaries in my possession, various years.

Holmgren, Virginia C. *Hilton Head: A Sea Island Chronicle*. Hilton Head Island: Hilton Head Island Publishing Company, 1959.

Hurlbut, Jesse Lyman, D. D. *Hurlbut's Story of the Bible for Young and Old*. Philadelphia: The John C. Winston Company, 1932.

The Island Packet, Hilton Head Island, SC: various issues.

Jones, Phil. *Cocktails and Prayers*. Canton, GA: Yawn's Publishing, 2017.

Kephart, Beth. *Handling the Truth: On the Writing of Memoir*. New York: Gotham Books, 2013.

Moore, Kay Sconyers. *Before the Bridge: A Memoir of Hilton Head Island*. Canton, GA: Yawn's Publishing, 2015.

Patton, Darryl. *America's Goat Man: Mr. Ches McCartney*. Gadsden, AL: Little River Press, 1994.

Rankin, Richard. *A New South Hunt Club: An Illustrated History of the Hilton Head Agricultural Society, 1917–1967*. Mount Holly, NC: Willow Hill Press, 2011.

Schneider, Pat. *Writing Alone and with Others*. New York: Oxford University Press, 2003.

Smith, Nelle and Ora. *Paradise: Memories of Hilton Head in the Early Days*. Chapel Hill, NC: The Chapel Hill Press, Inc., 2018.

The State, Columbia, SC, various editions, 1956.

Tazewell, Charles, illustrated by Katherine Evans. *The Littlest Angel*. New York: Grosset & Dunlap, 1946.

Welty, Eudora. *One Writer's Beginnings*. Cambridge, MA: Harvard University Press, 1984.

Wilwerding, Walter J. *Punda: The Tiger Horse*. New York: MacMillan and Company, 1937.

Wister, Owen. *The Virginian: A Horseman of the Plains*. New York: Scribner Book Company, 1902.

Wyss, Johann. *The Swiss Family Robinson*. New York: Grosset & Dunlap, Inc., 1949.

About the Author

Avary Hack Doubleday moved with her family to Hilton Head Island in June 1950, at the age of five. The Hacks were one of the few white families living permanently on the Island. Modern conveniences such as electricity, telephones, and even medical services were not part of Island life. Avary lived there until graduating from Agnes Scott College in 1967. After earning an MBA in accounting she enjoyed a career in accounting and finance in Atlanta, Georgia. In 2000, she moved with her husband, Gerry, to Highlands, North Carolina. Since retiring, she has volunteered with numerous nonprofit organizations, serving on several boards in both Atlanta and Highlands, including libraries and environmental organizations. She also enjoys reading; traveling, particularly in Africa; birdwatching; and writing. This memoir of her life on Hilton Head Island before the bridge is her first published work. Avary and Gerry split their time between Highlands and Greenwood, South Carolina.